790 Miles

790 Miles

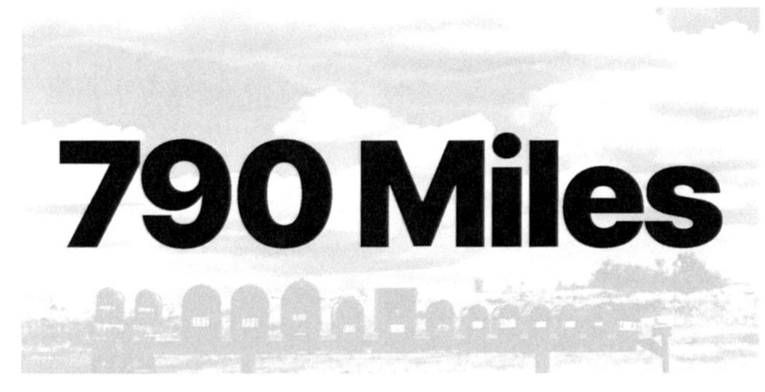

Otto Kitsinger

A drive across mostly rural southern Idaho and back,
790 miles,
35 hours,
in chronological order.

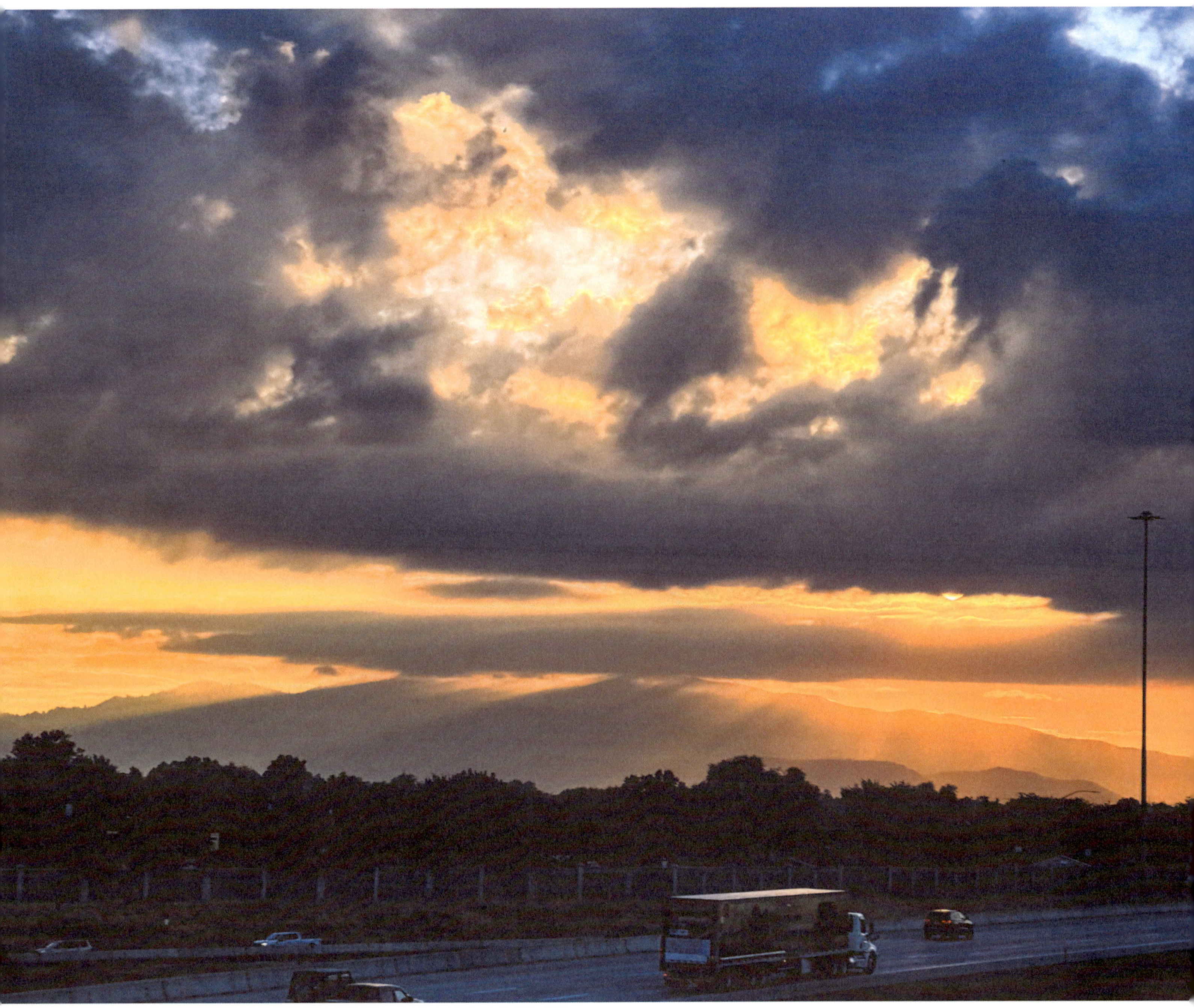

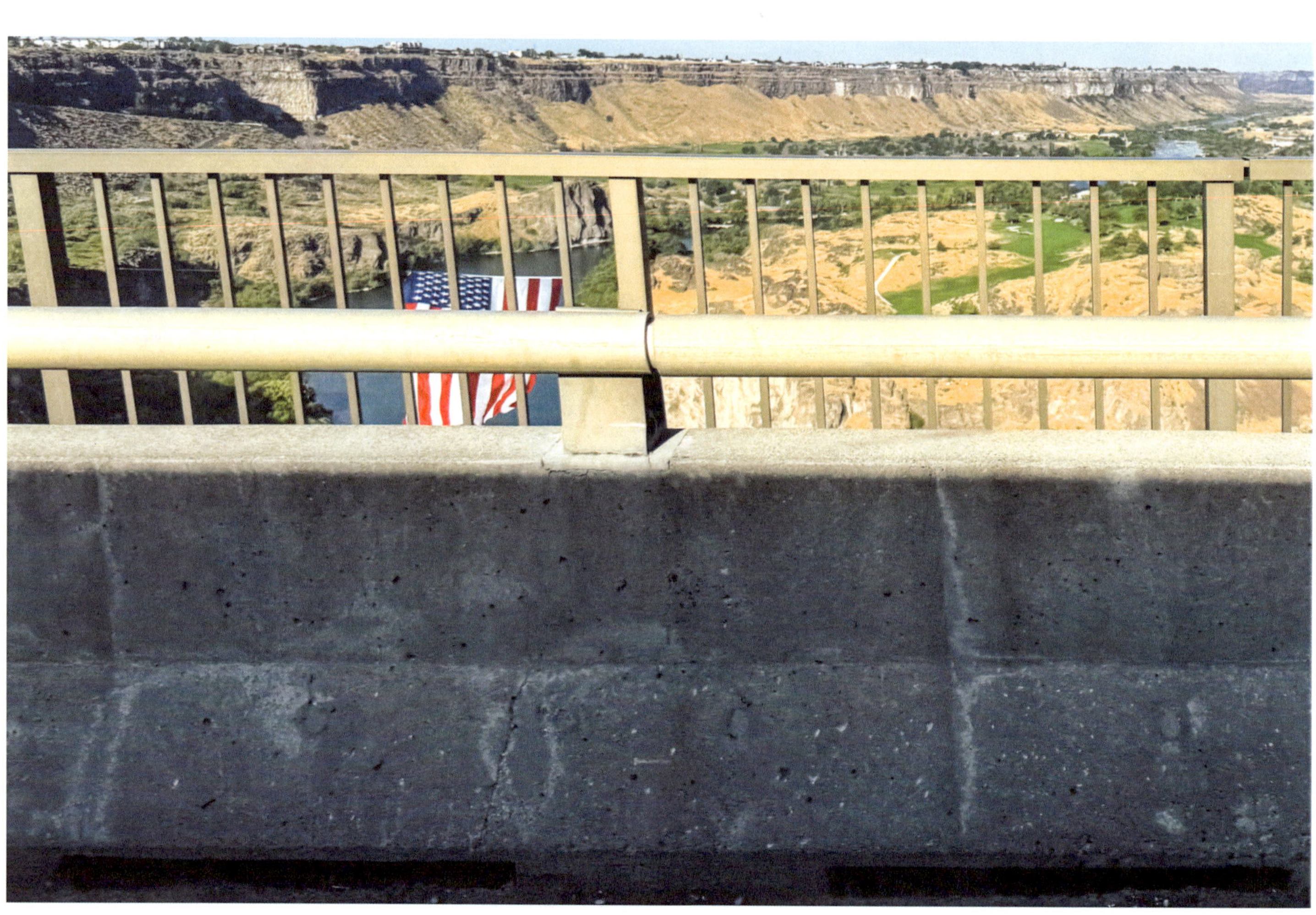

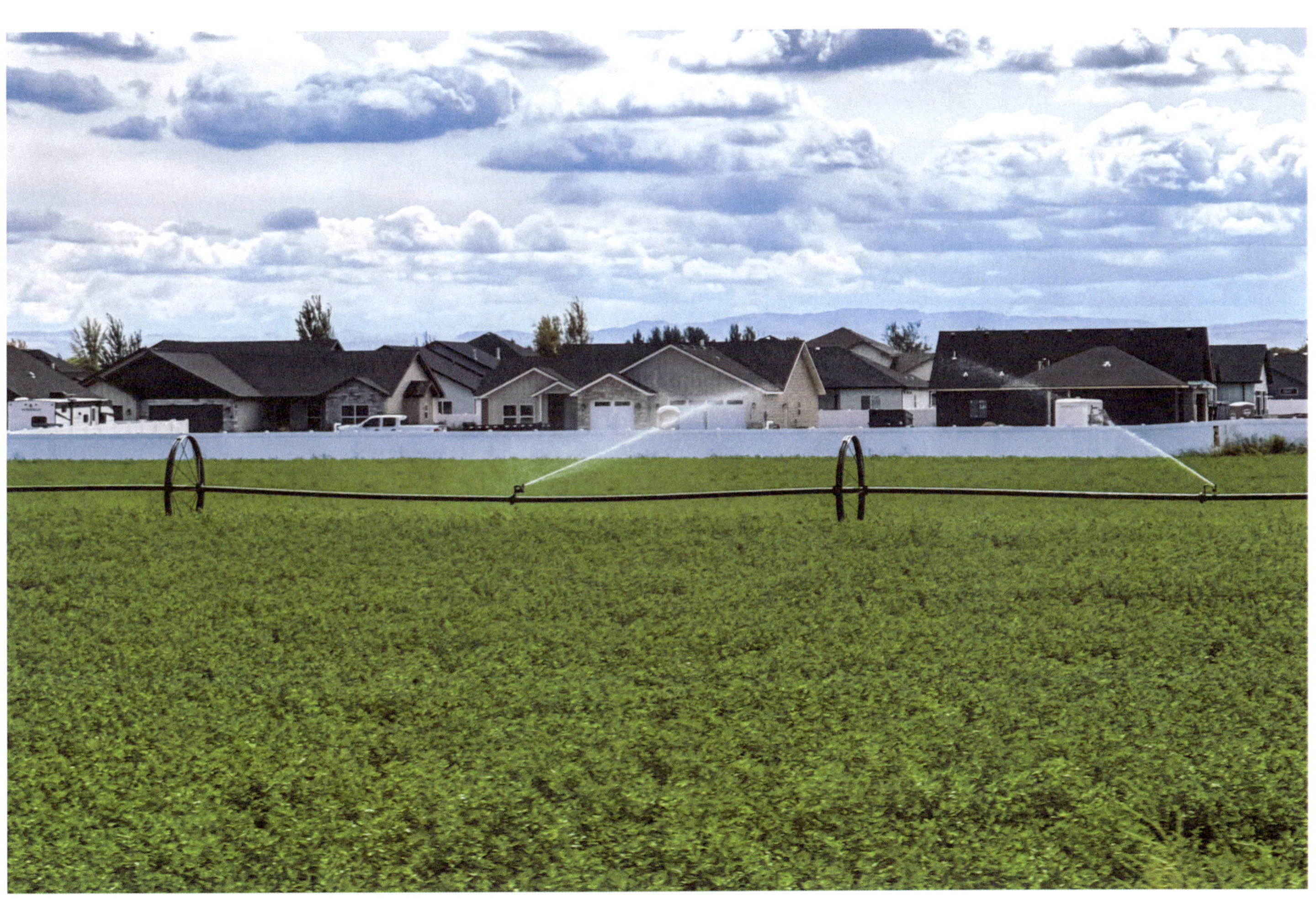

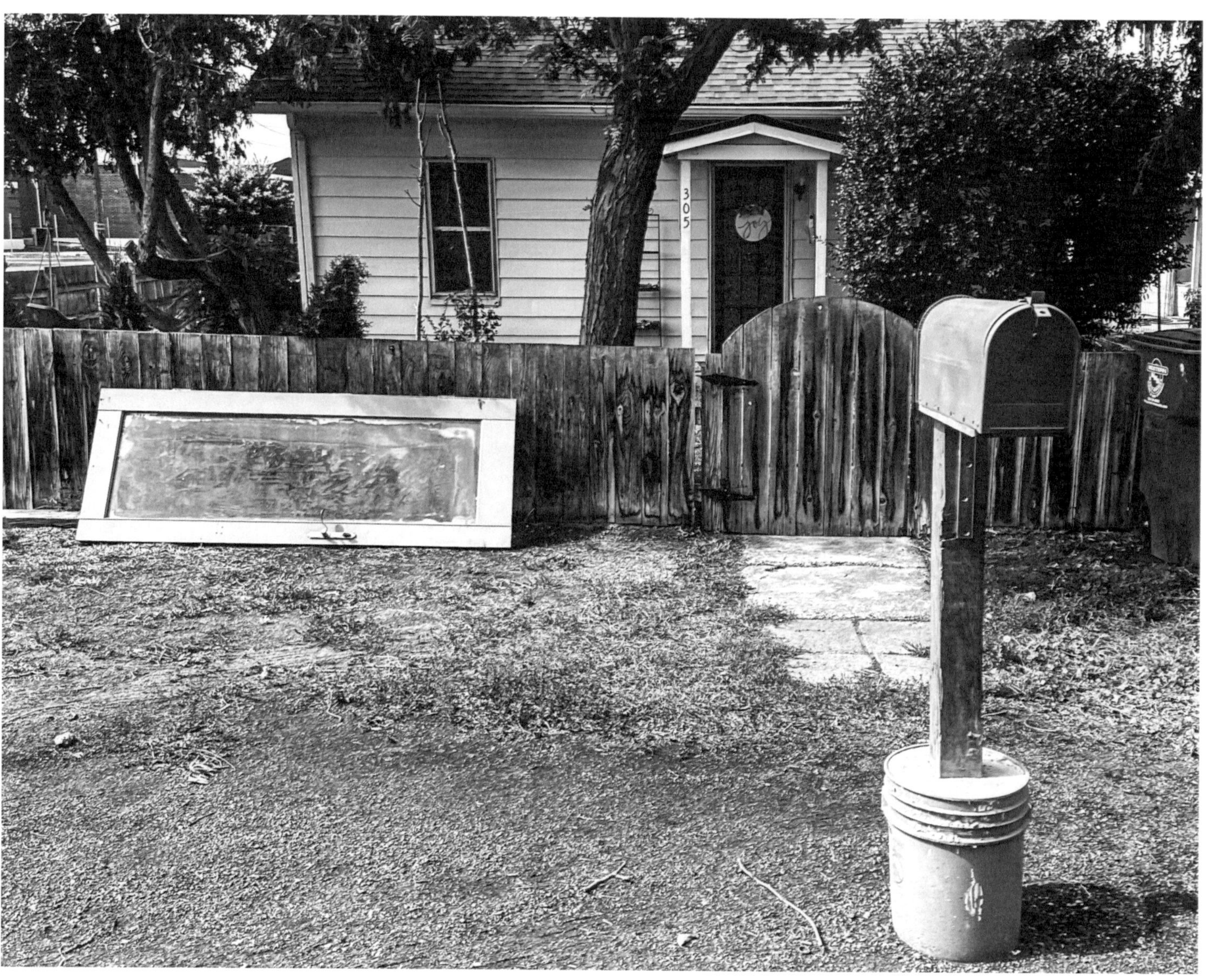

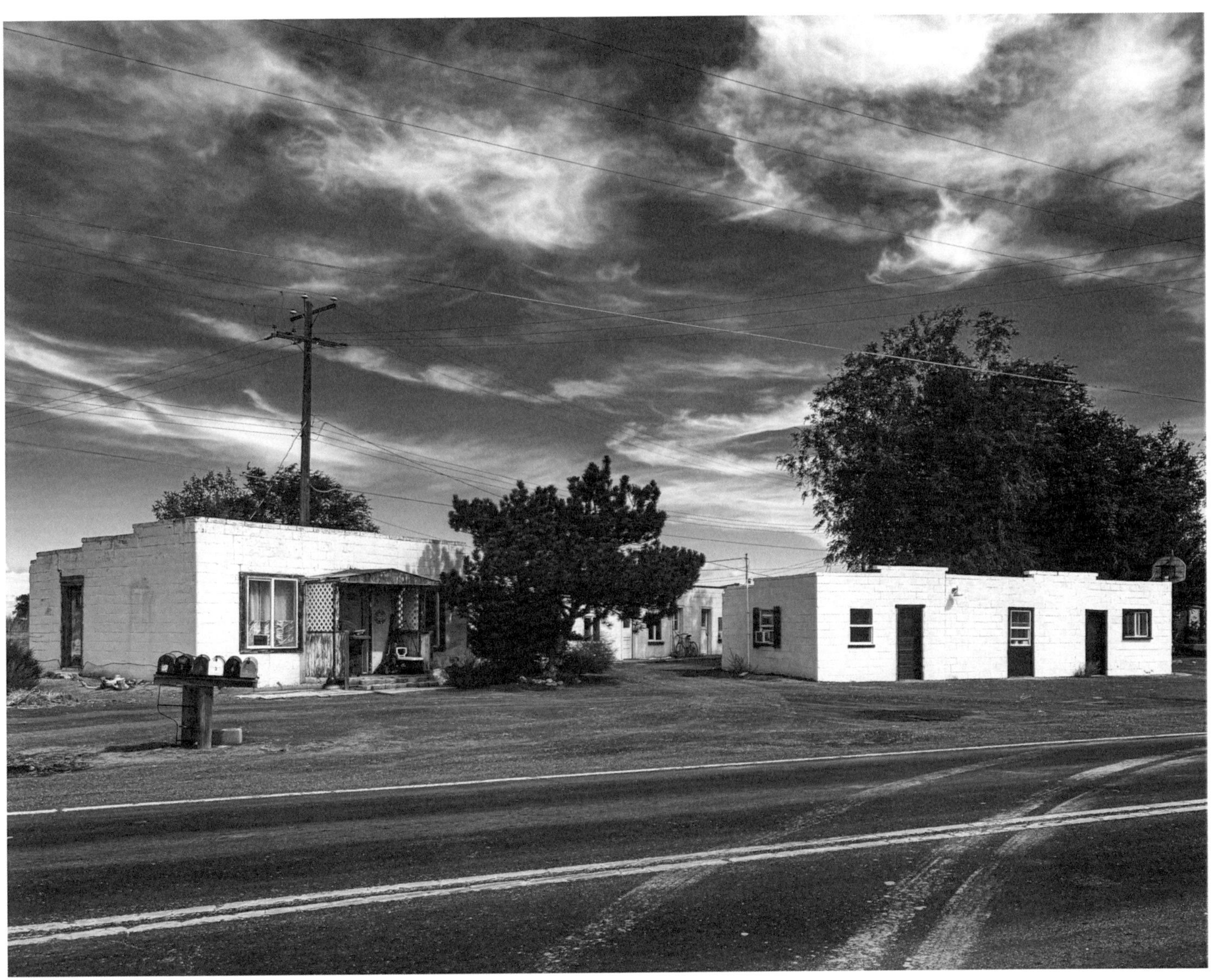

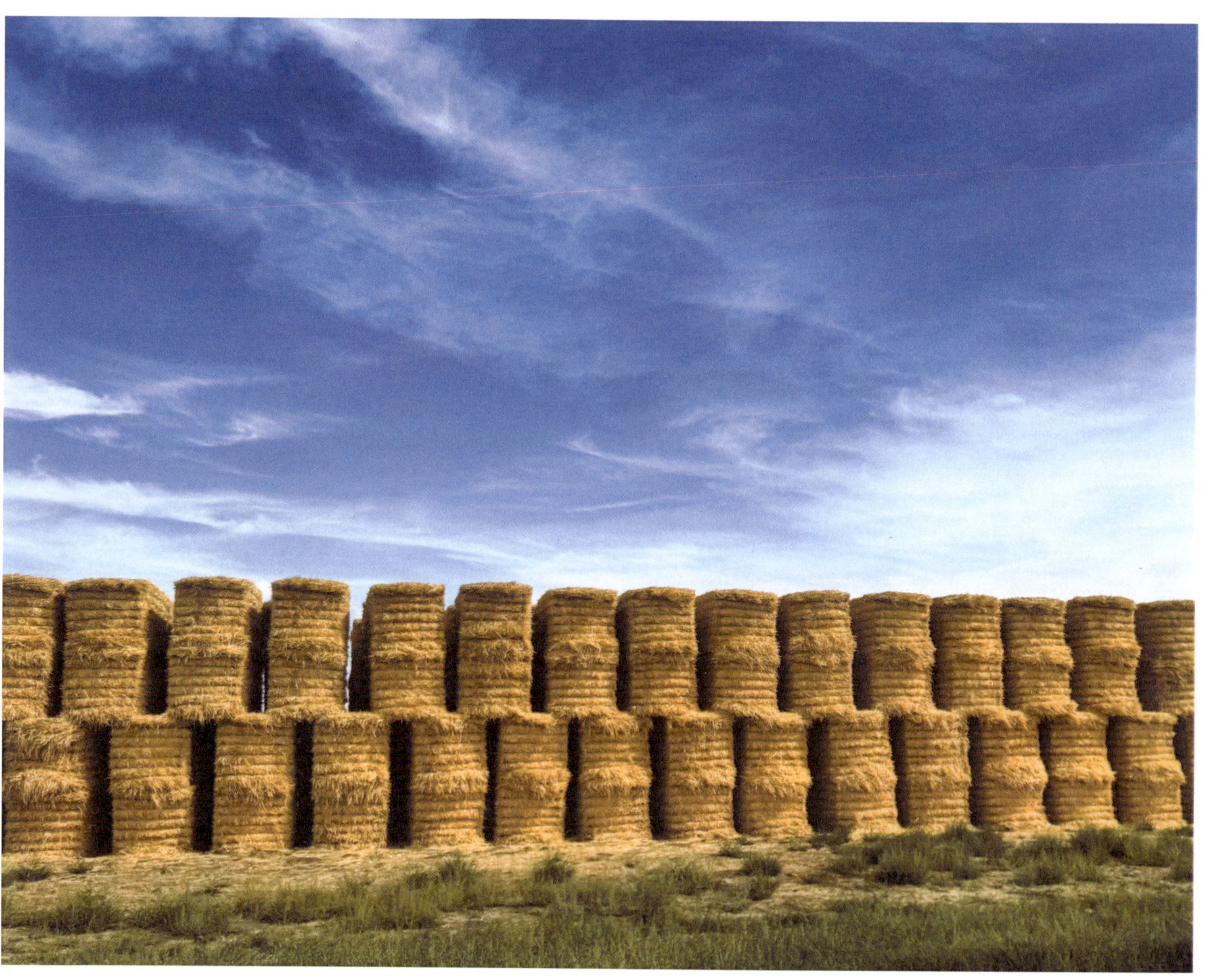

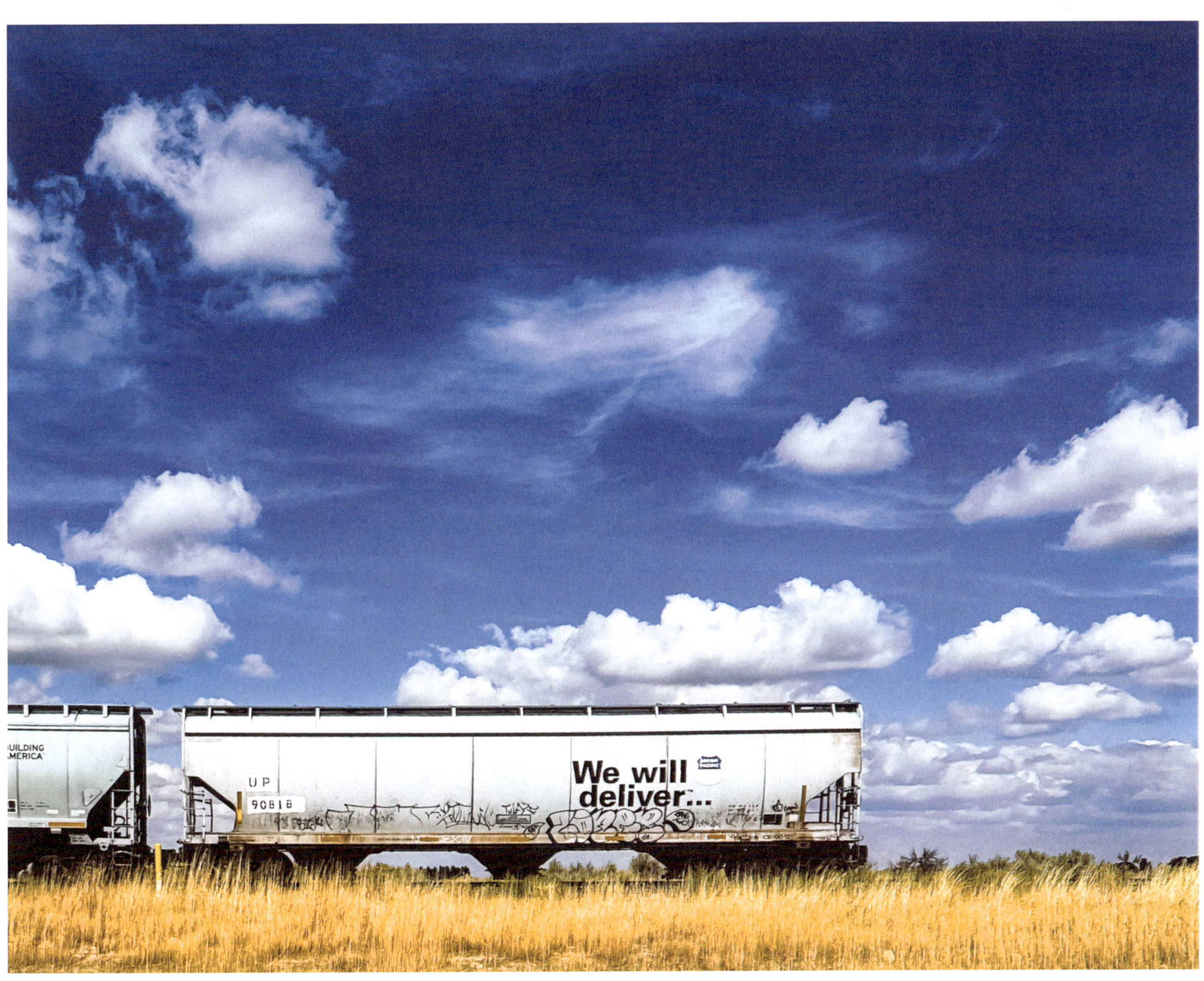
BUILDING
AMERICA
UP
90818
We will
deliver...

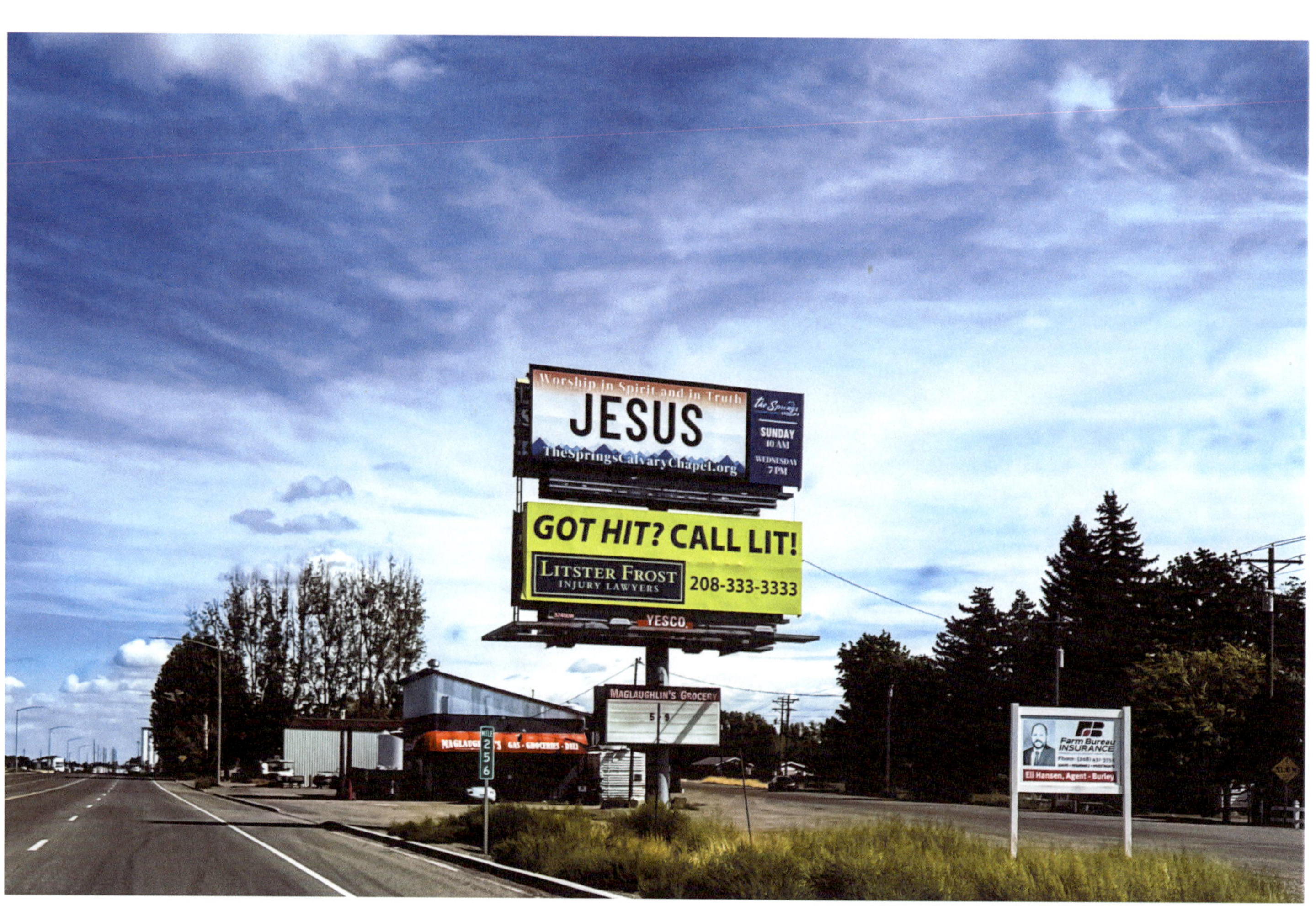
Worship in Spirit and in Truth
JESUS
TheSpringsCalvaryChapel.org
The Springs
SUNDAY
10 AM
WEDNESDAY
7 PM
GOT HIT? CALL LIT!
LITSTER FROST
INJURY LAWYERS
208-333-3333
YESCO
Maglaughlin's Grocery
MAGLAUGHLIN'S GAS · GROCERIES · DELI
MILE 256
Farm Bureau
INSURANCE
Eli Hansen, Agent - Burley

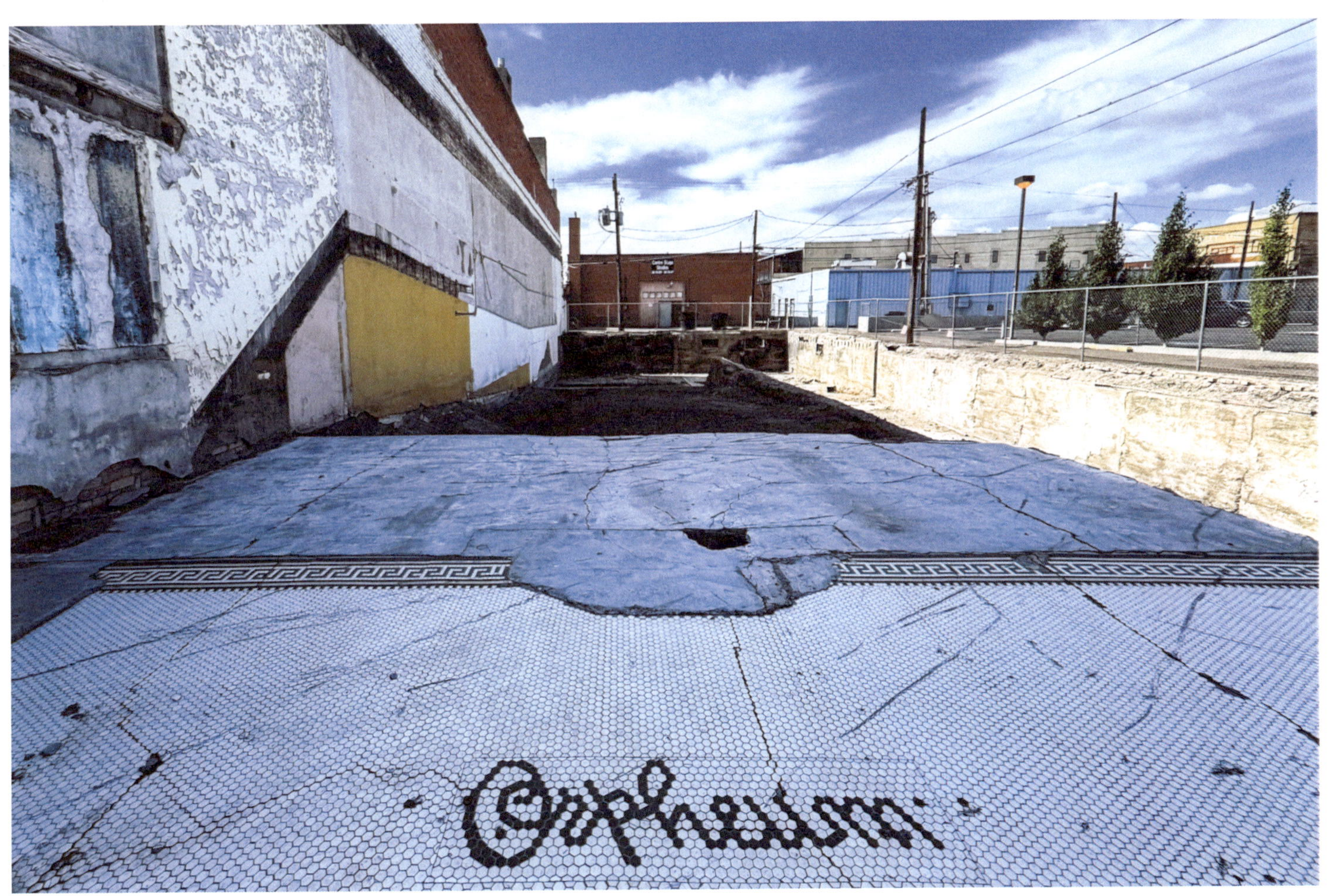
Orpheum

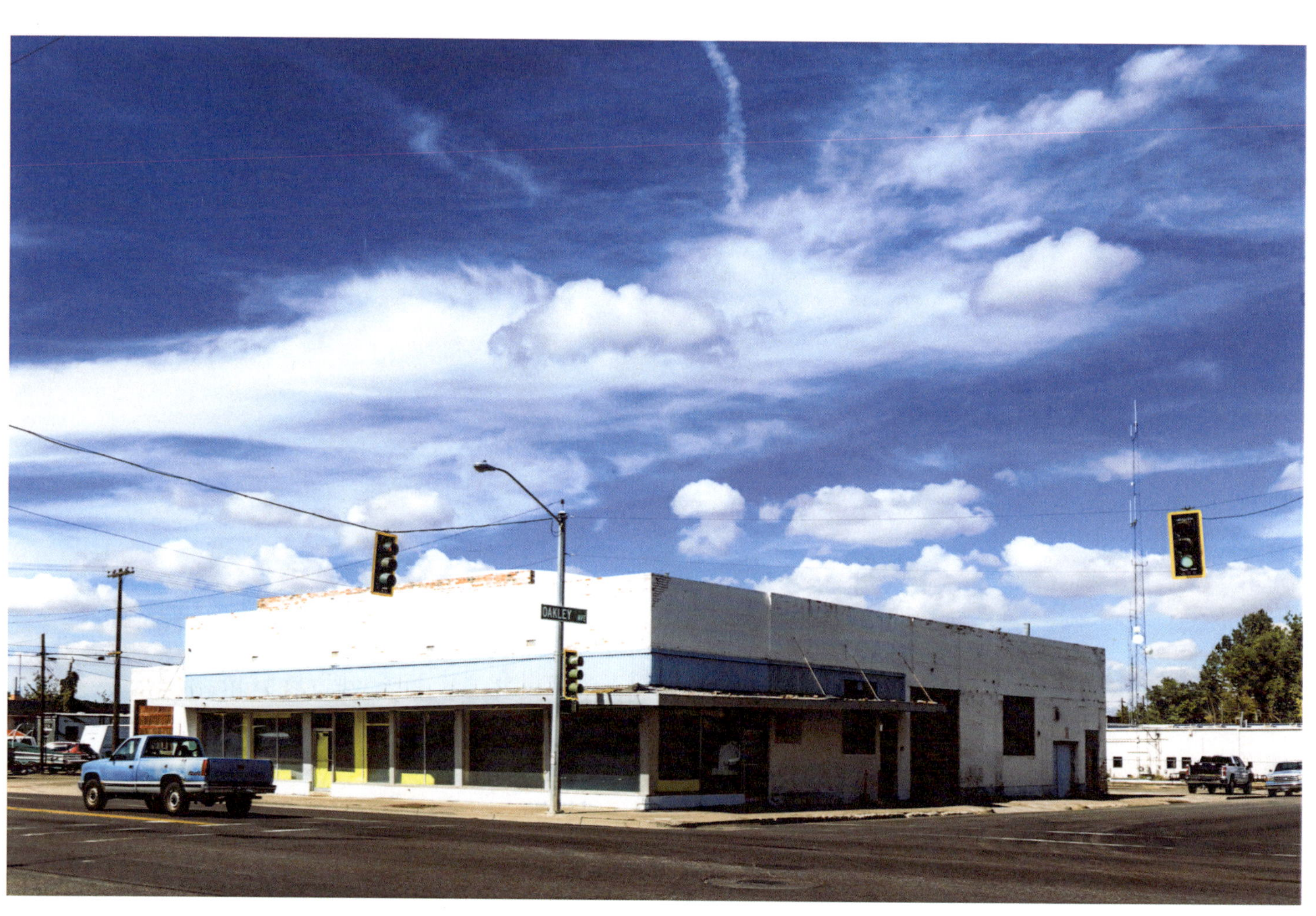

OAKLEY AVE

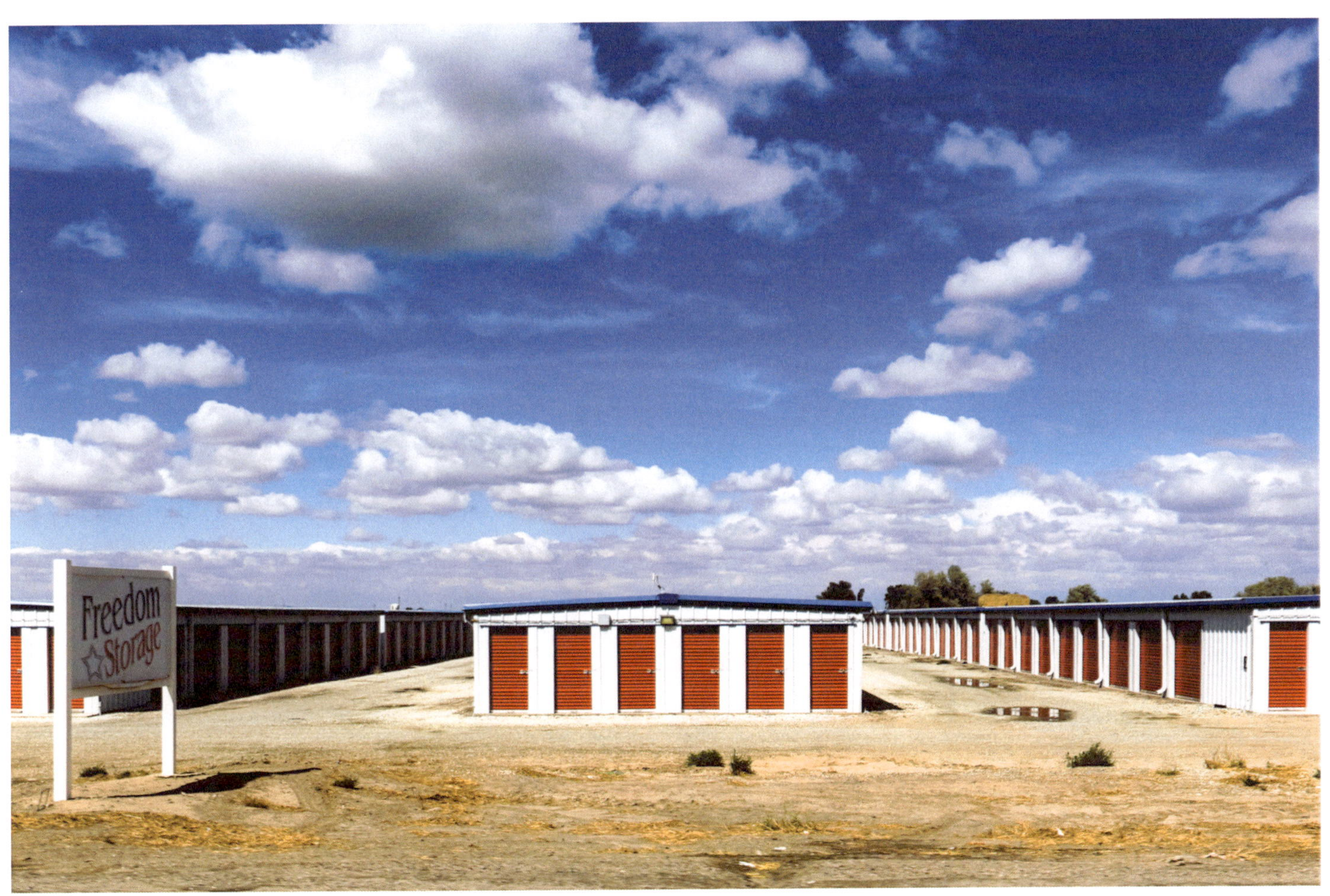

Freedom
Storage

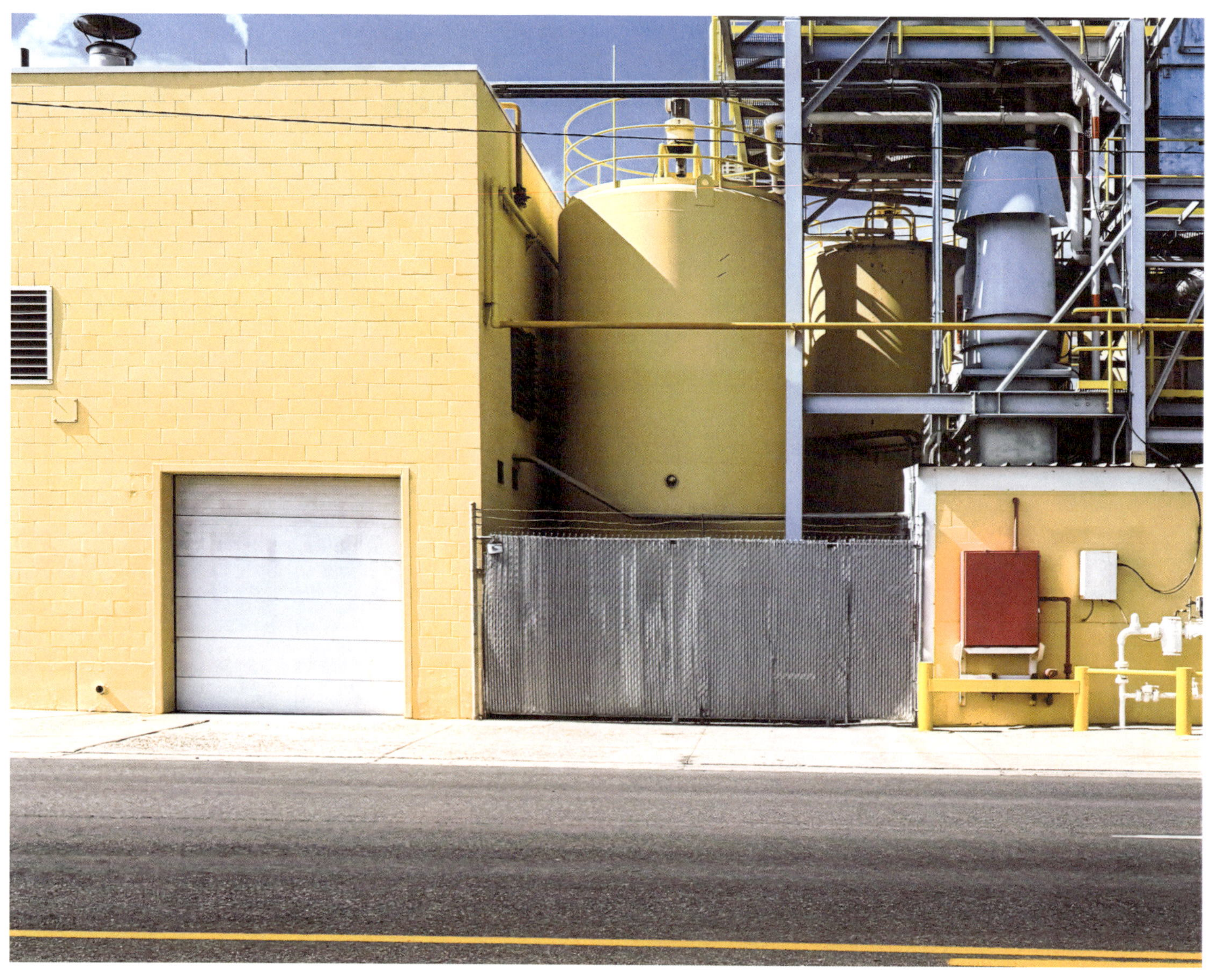

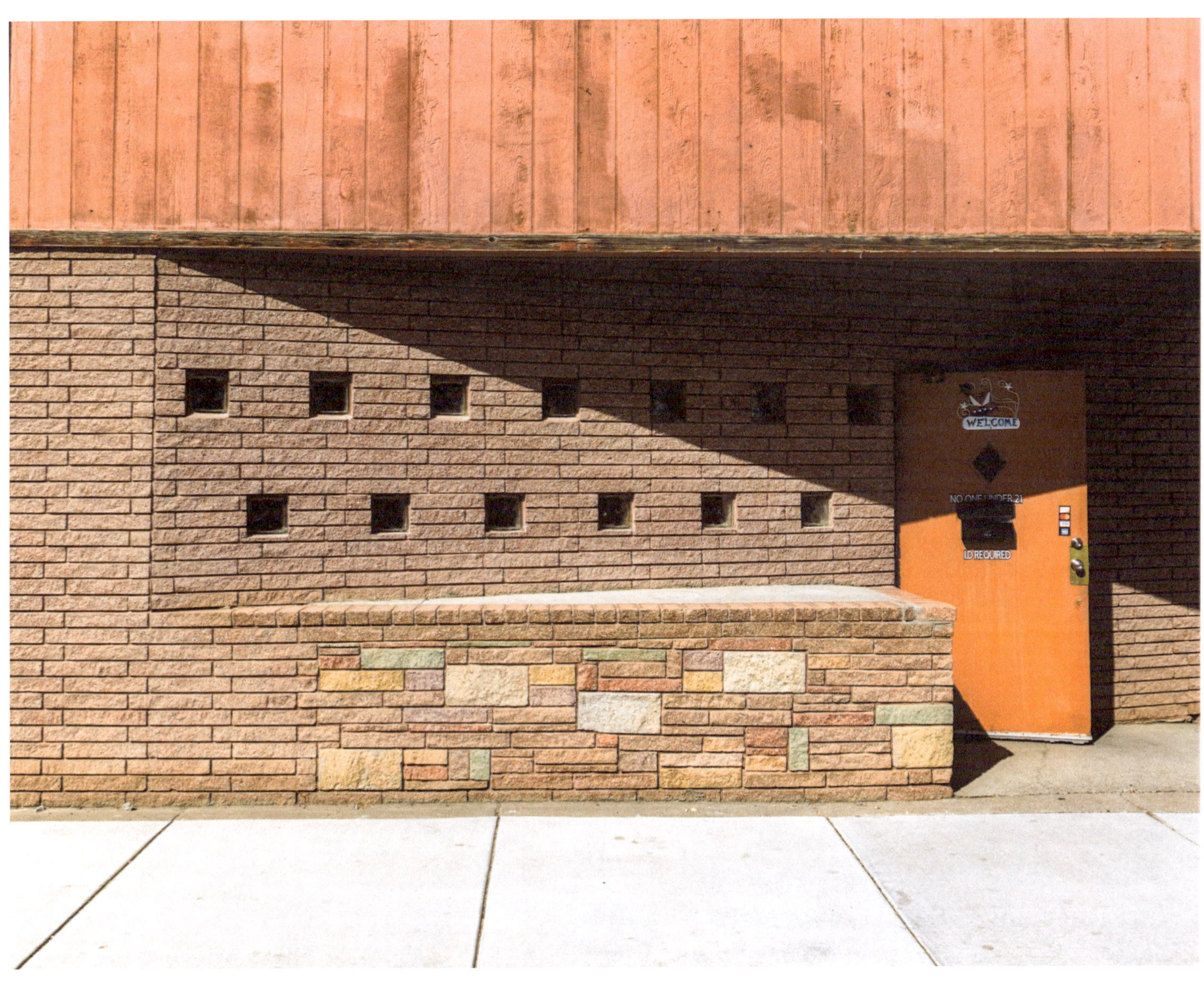

WELCOME
NO ONE UNDER 21
I.D. REQUIRED

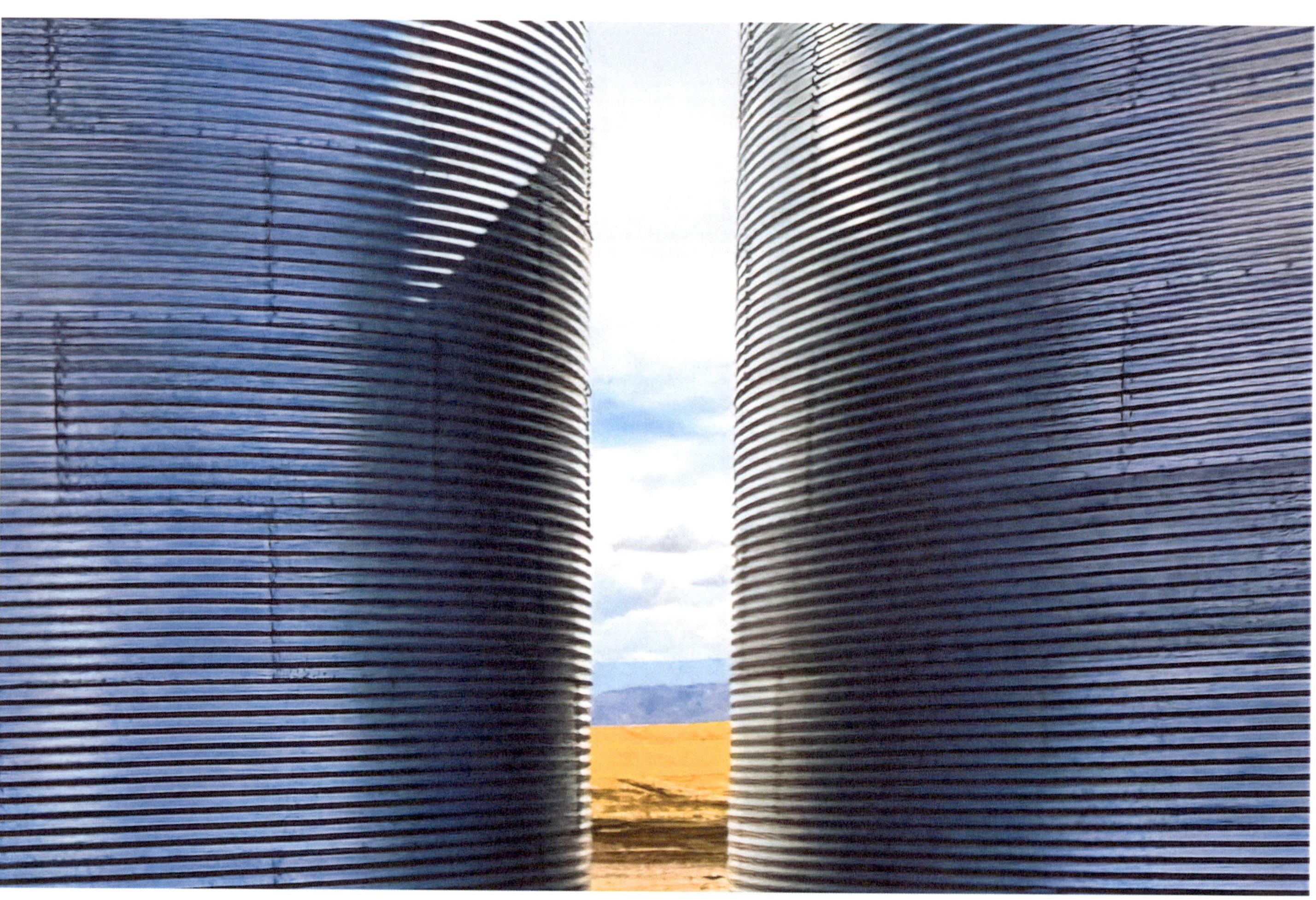

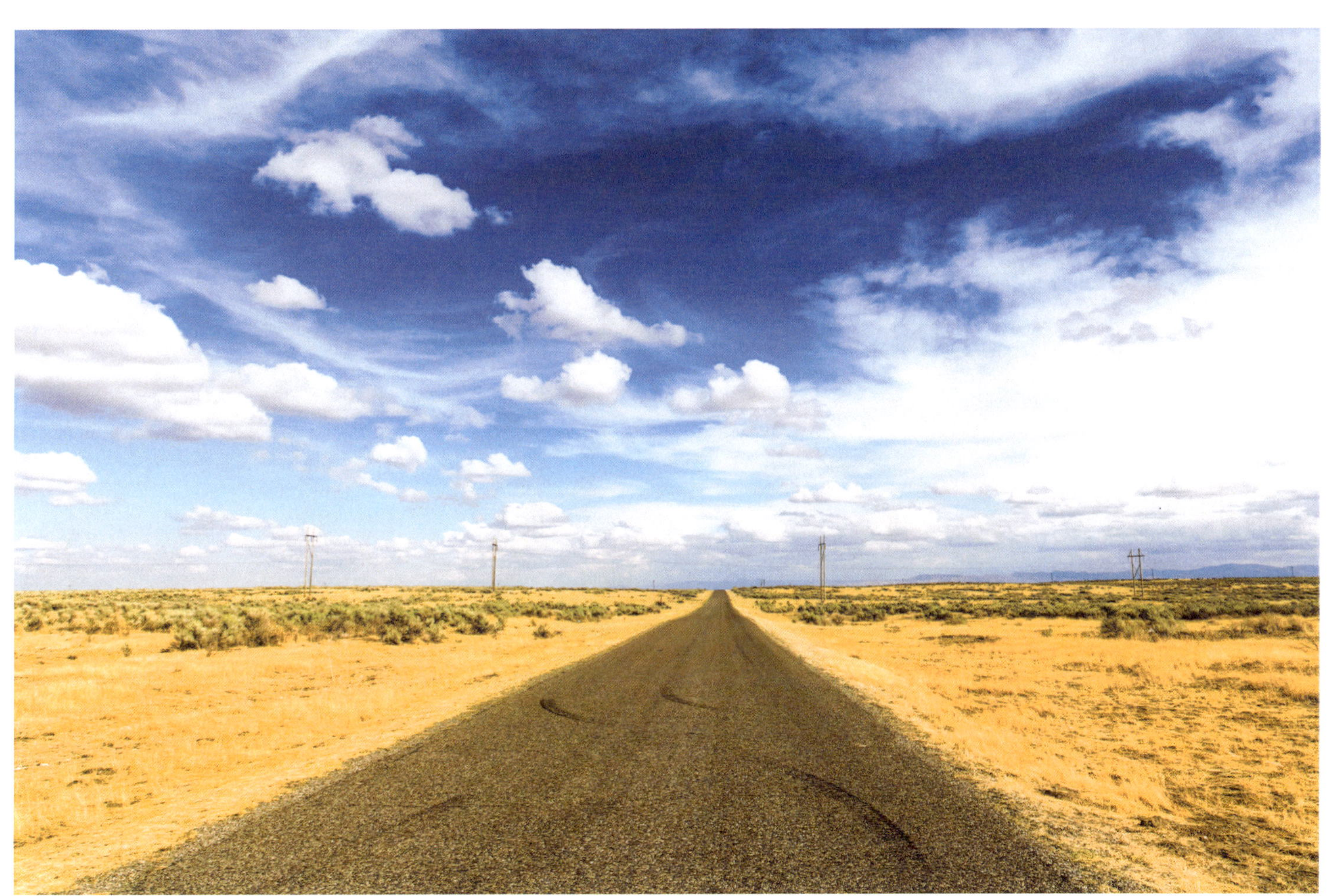

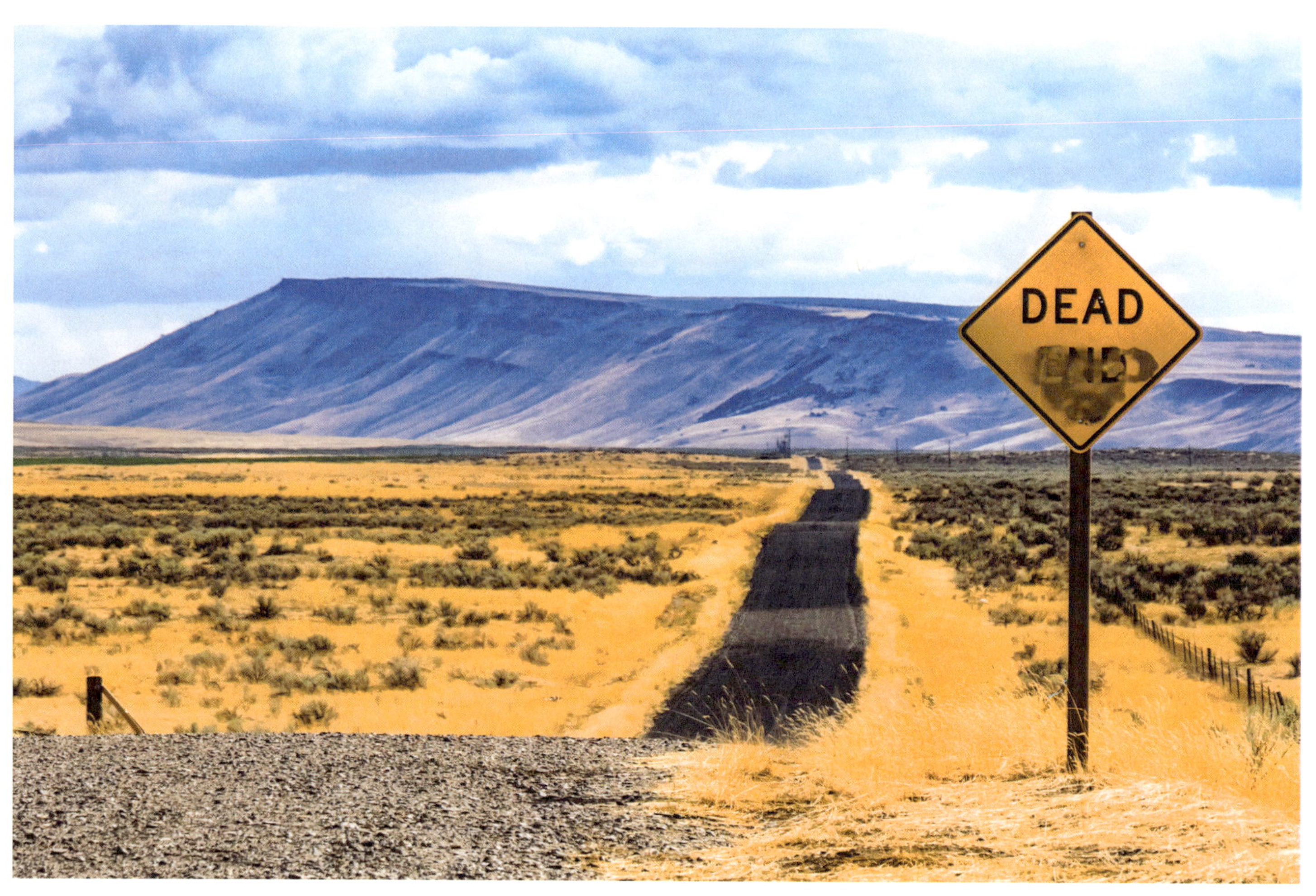

DEAD
END

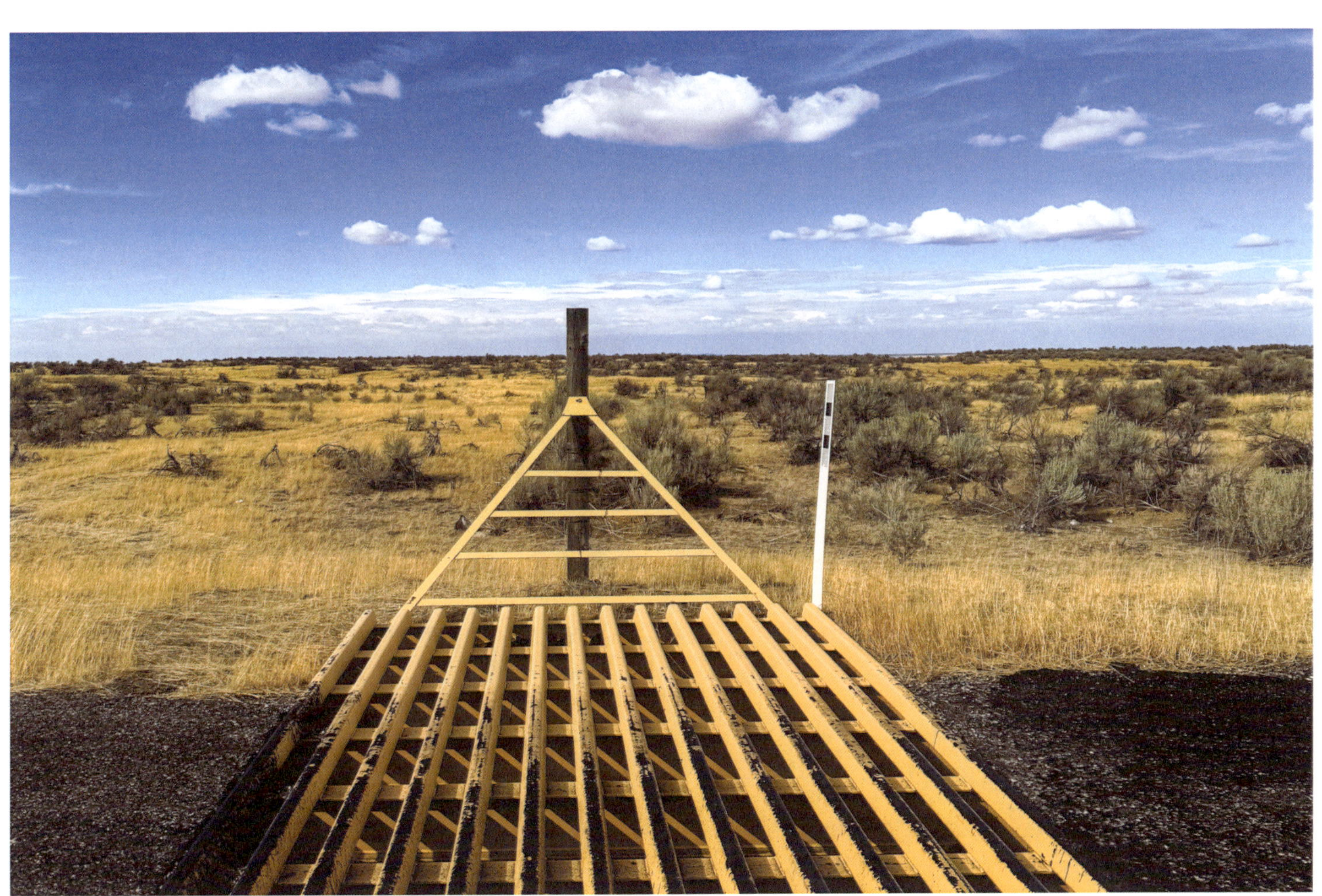

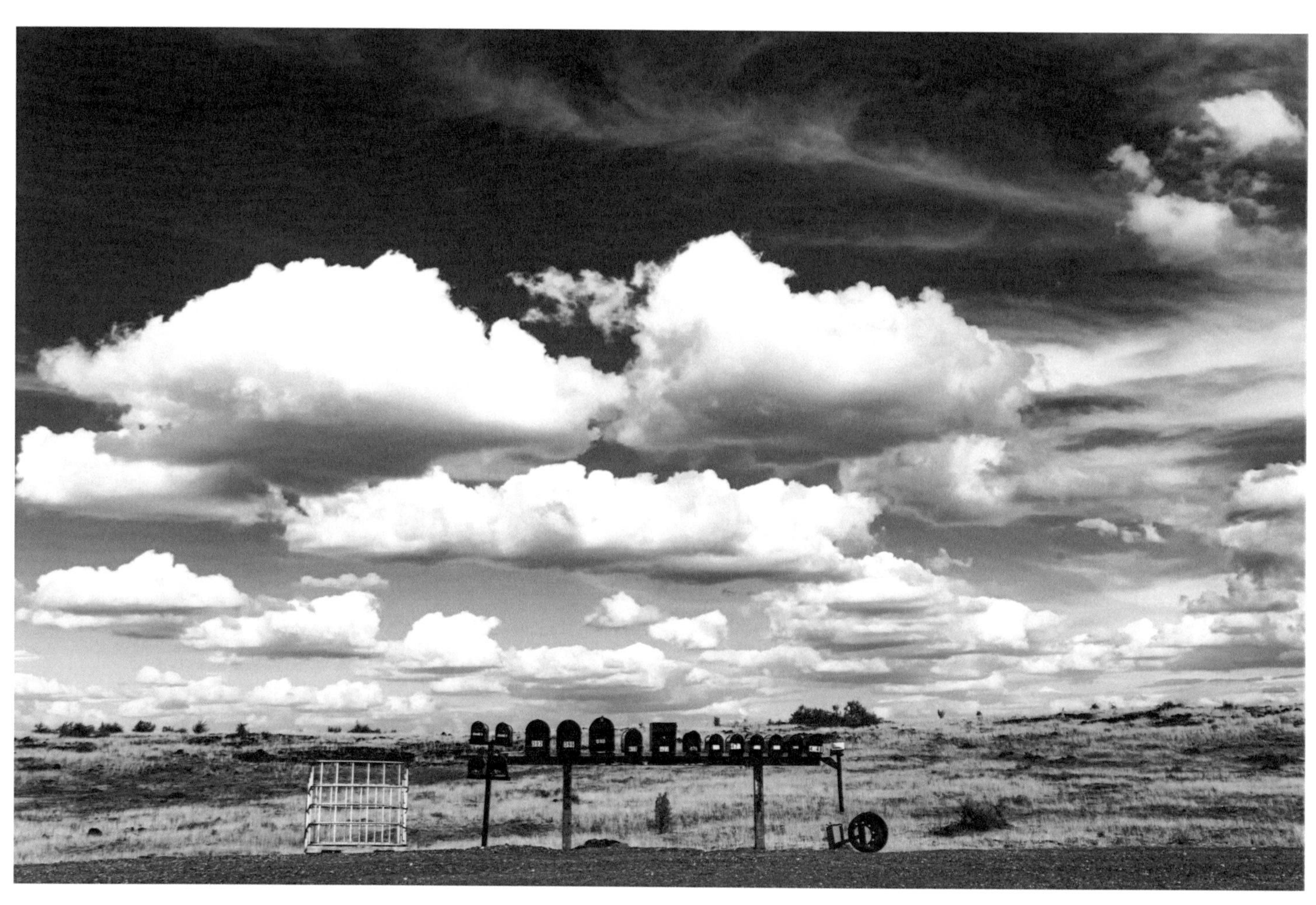

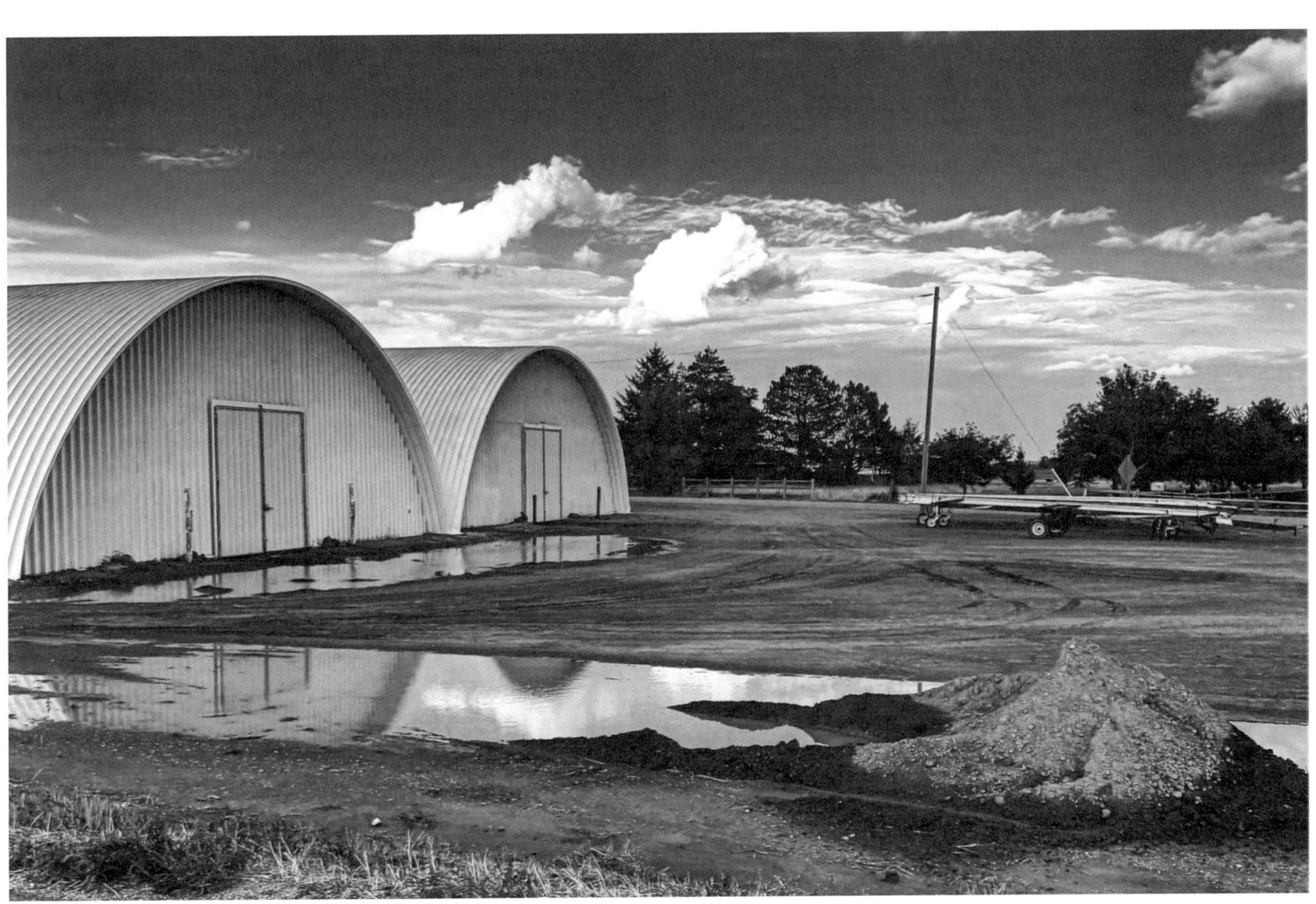

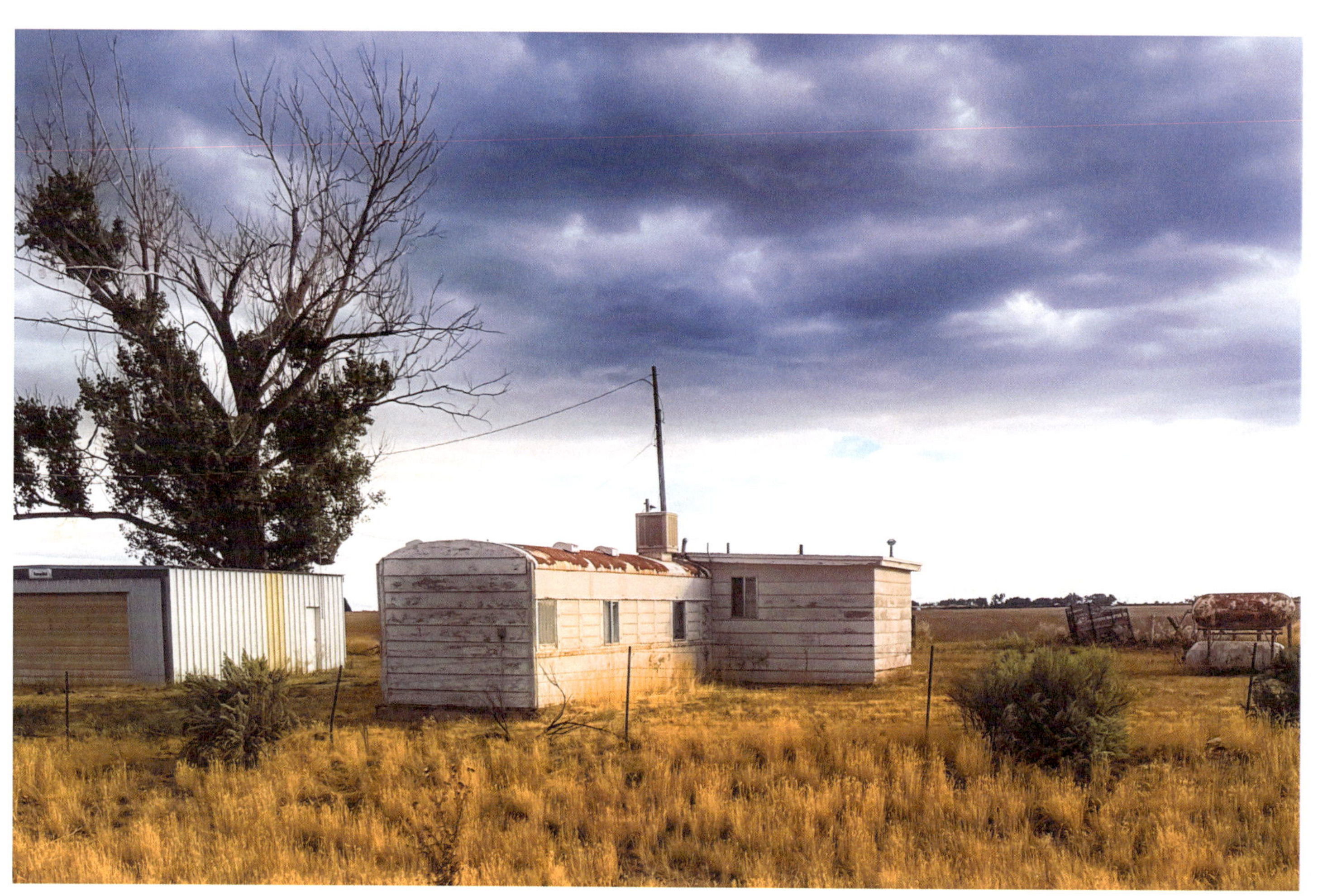

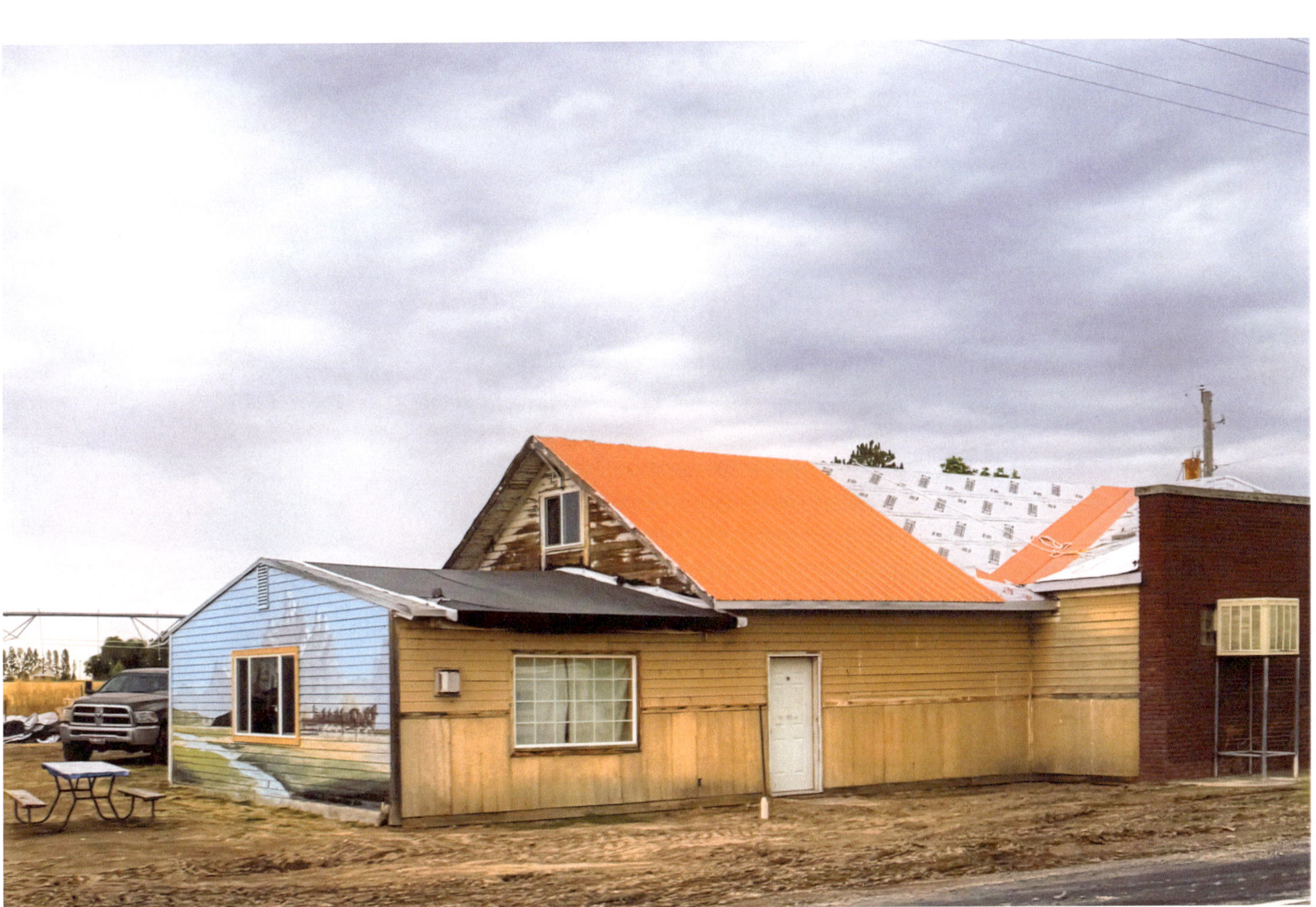

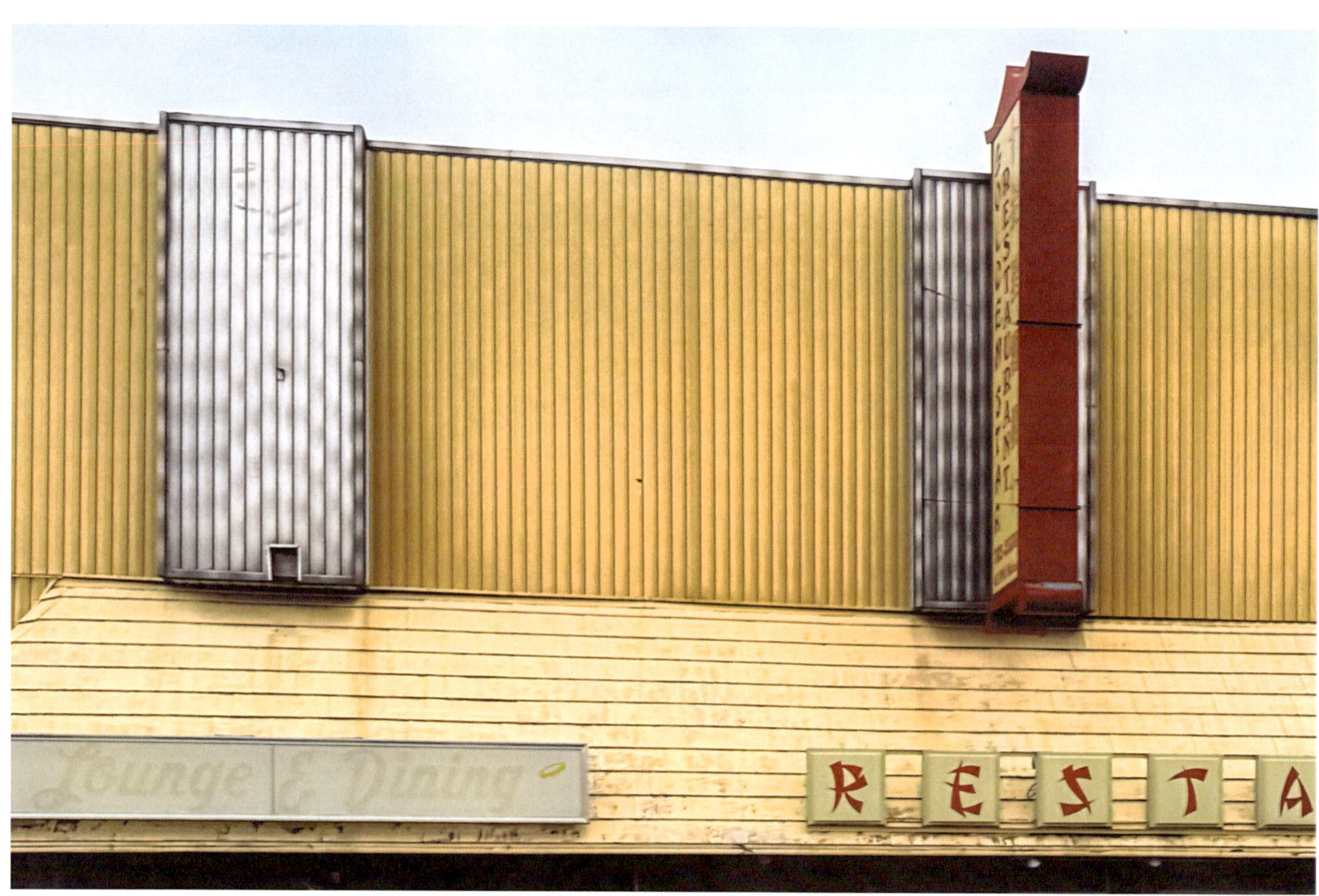

Lounge & Dining
RESTA
RESTAURANT

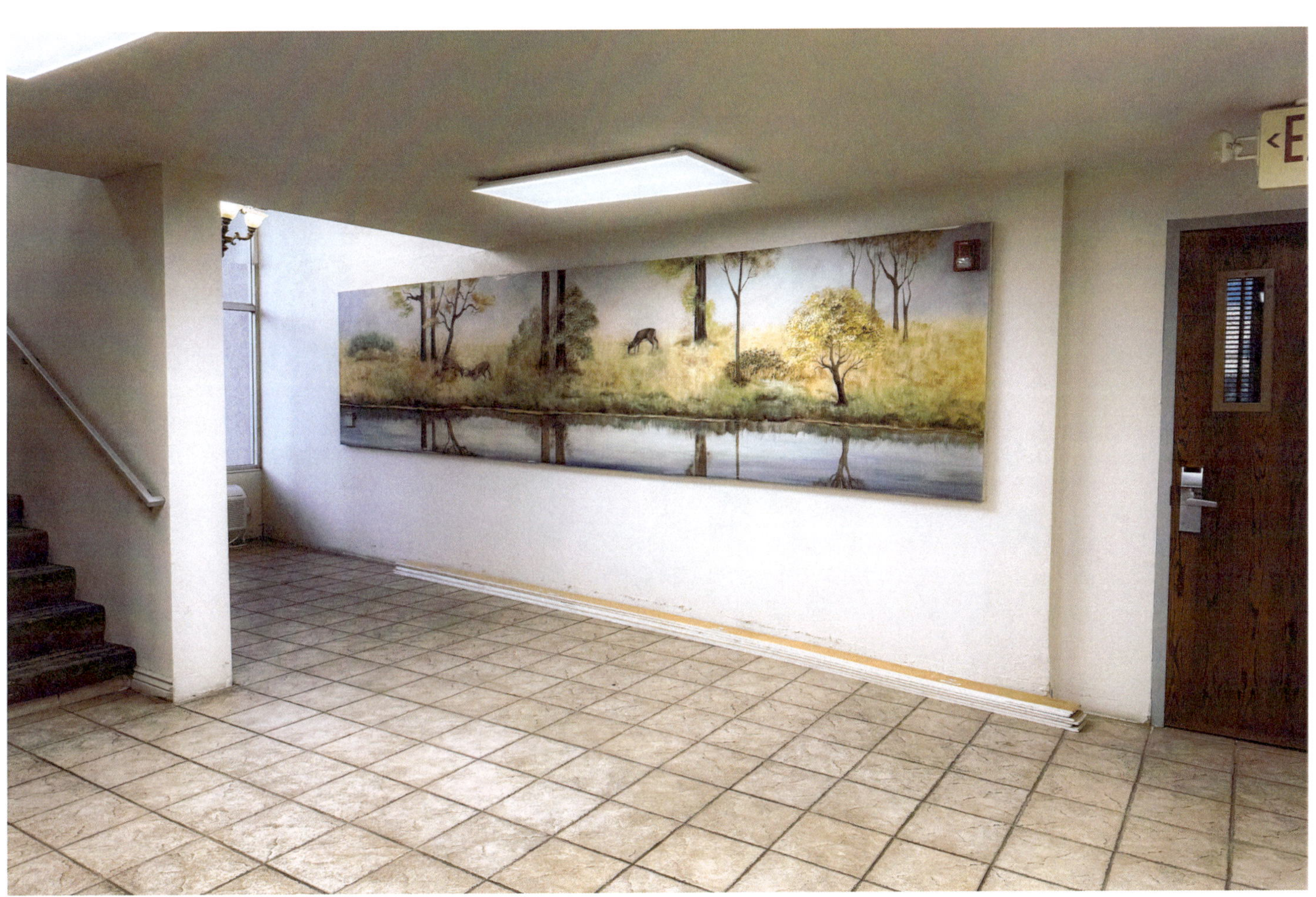

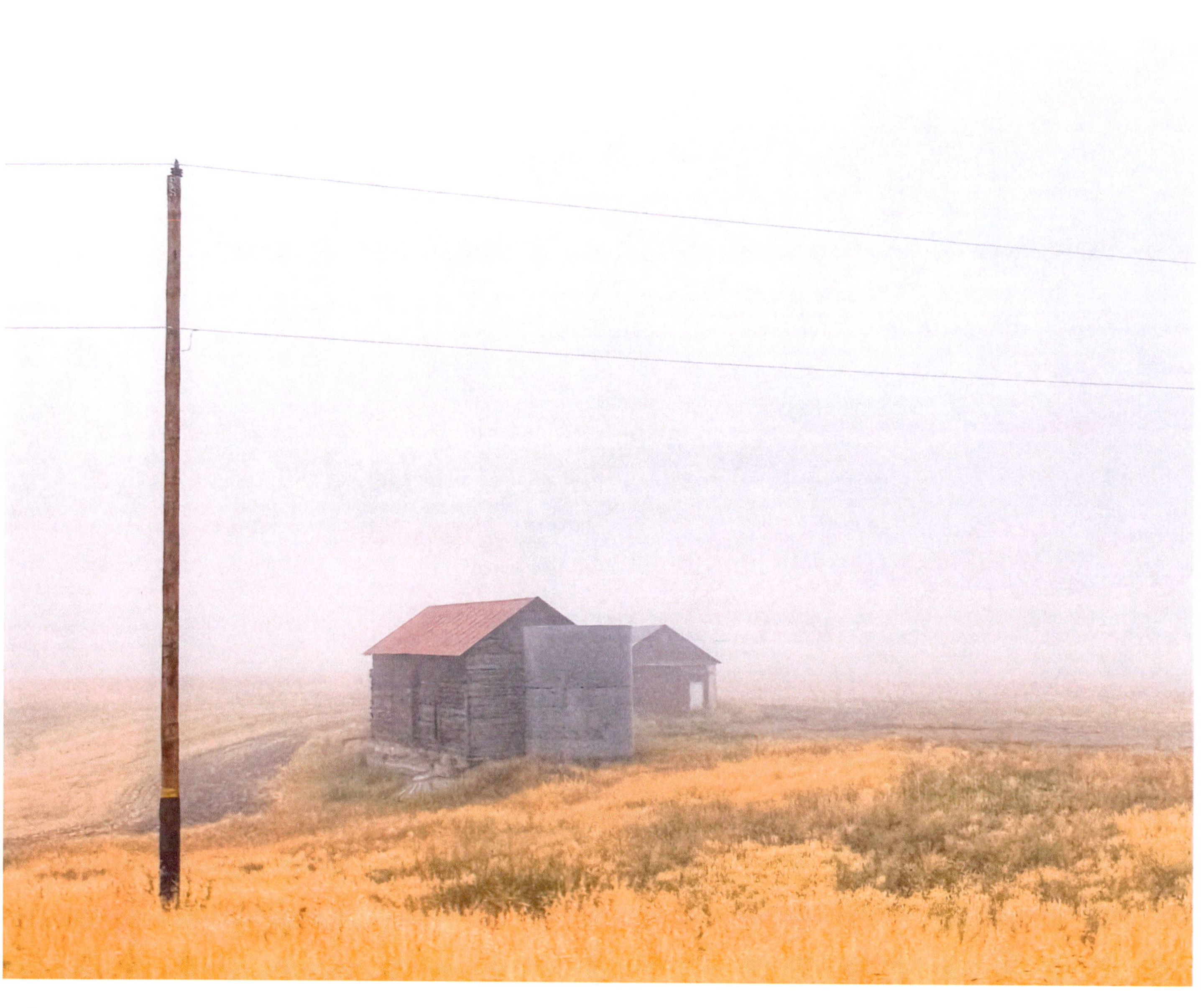

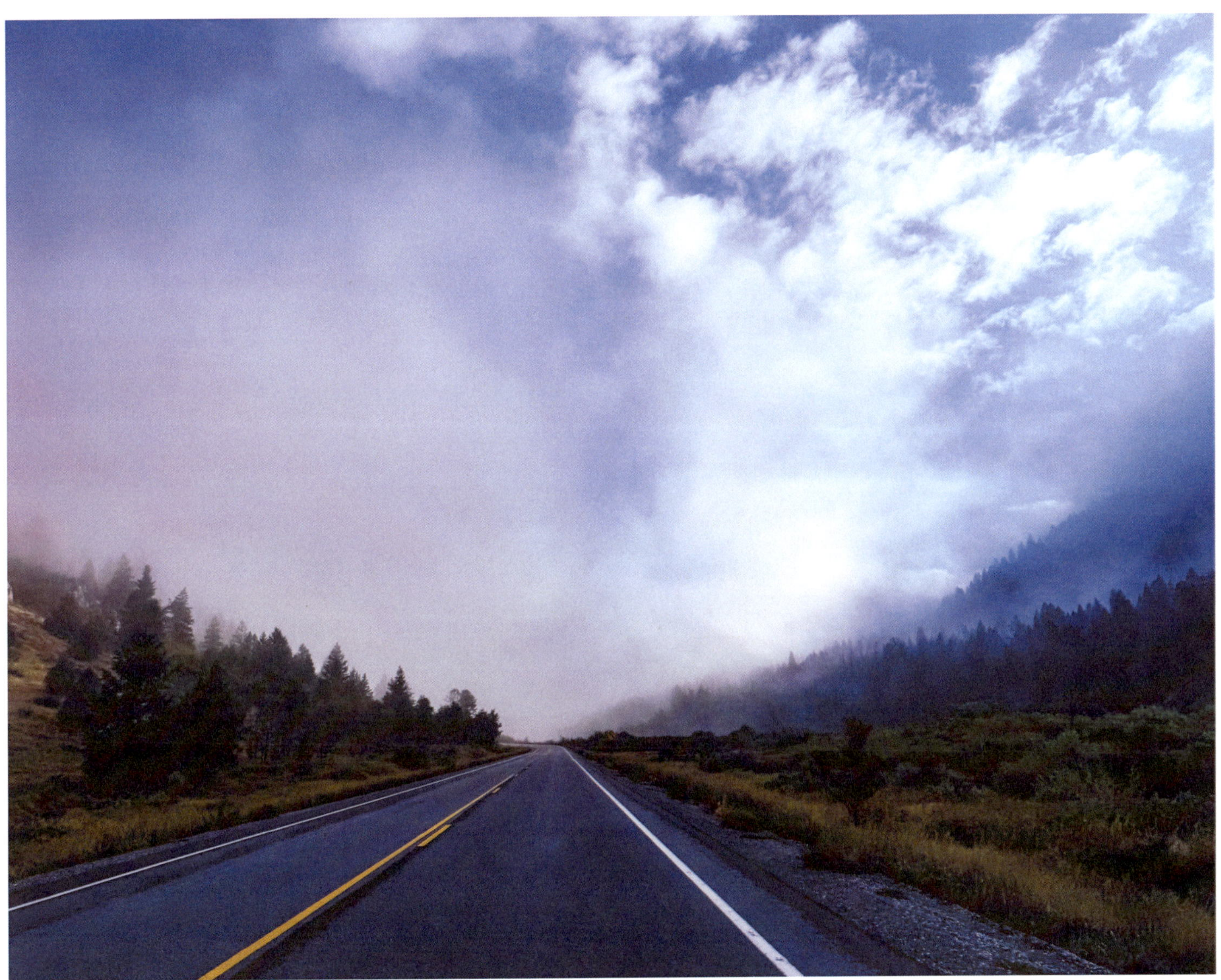

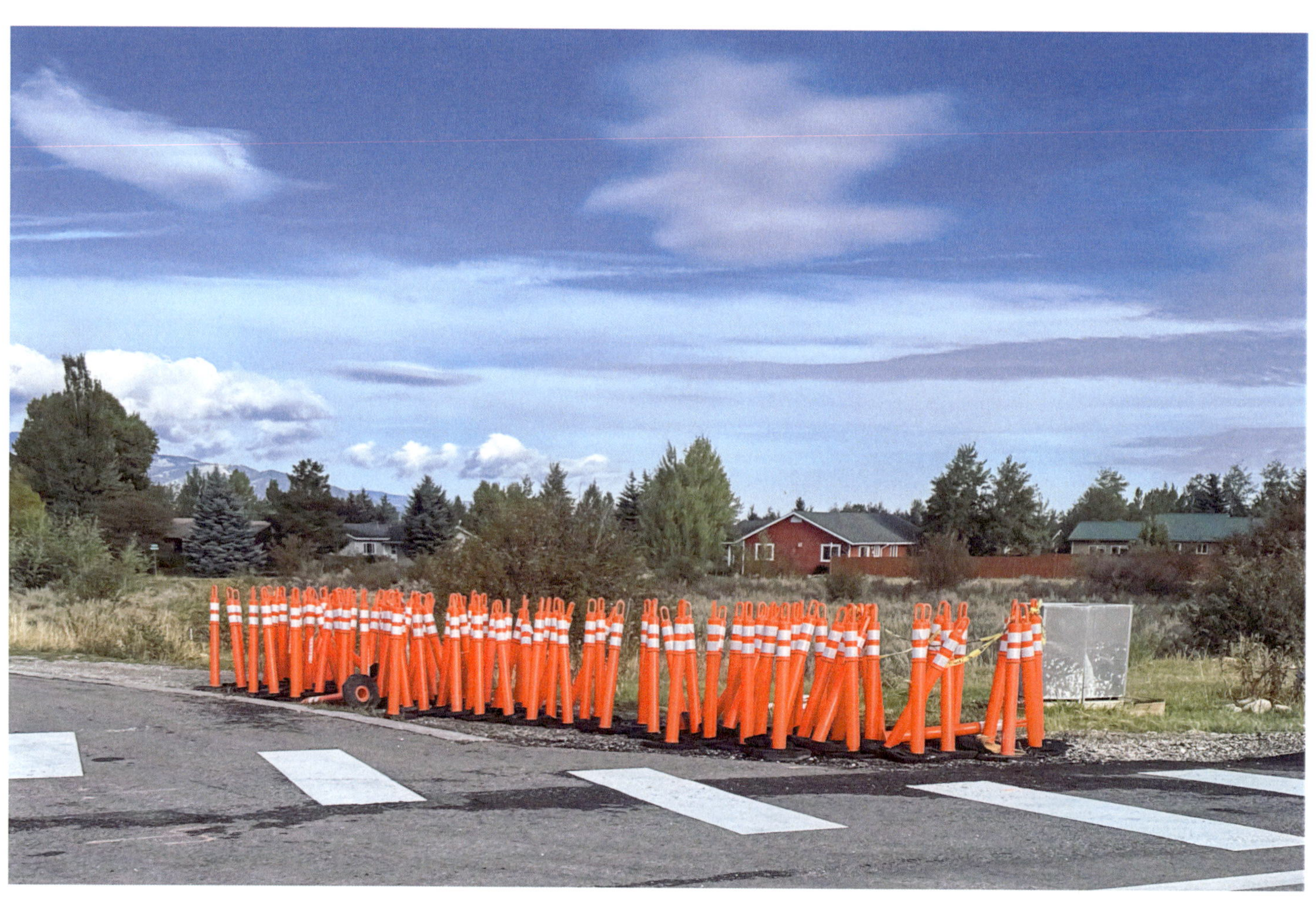

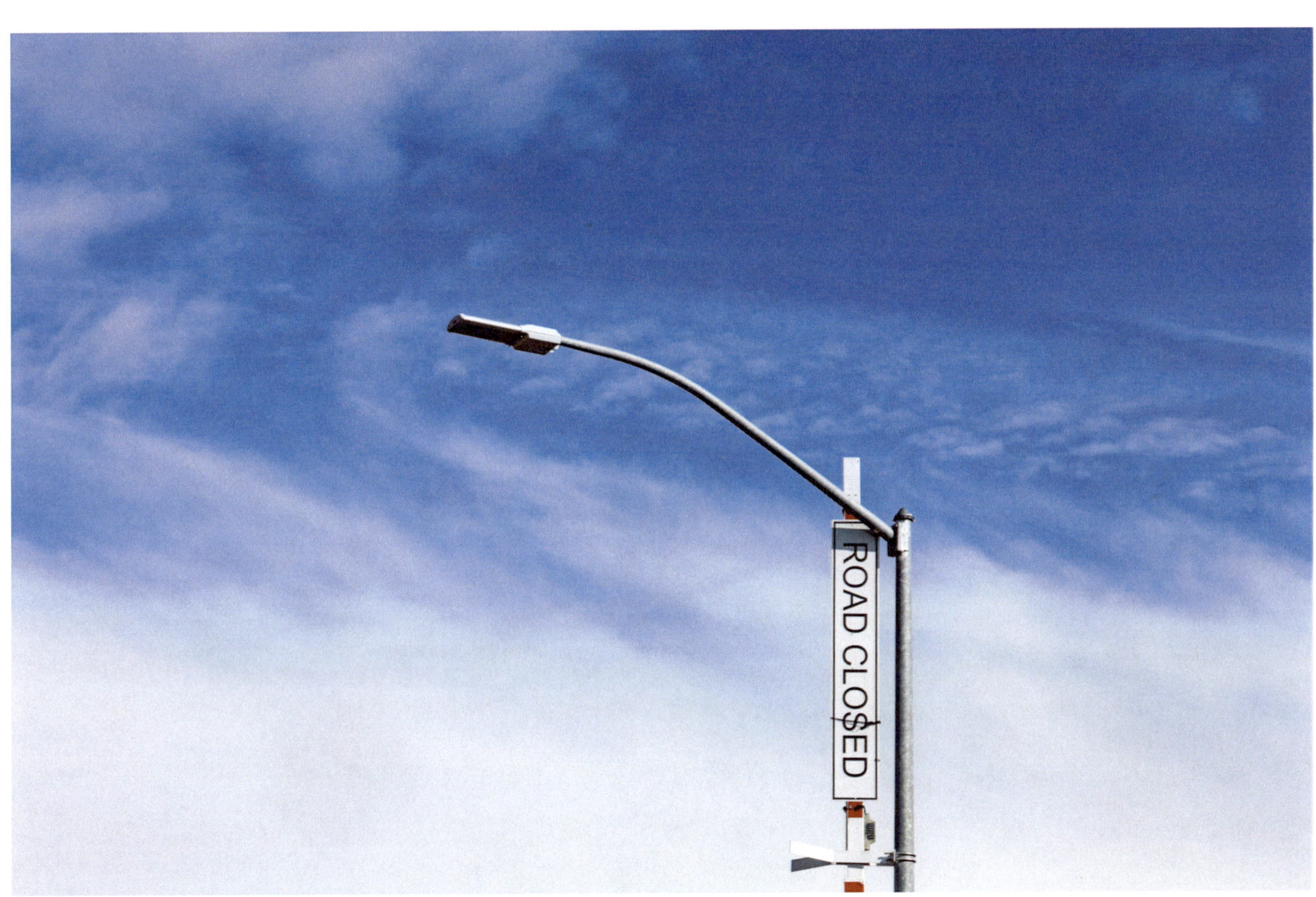

ROAD CLO$ED

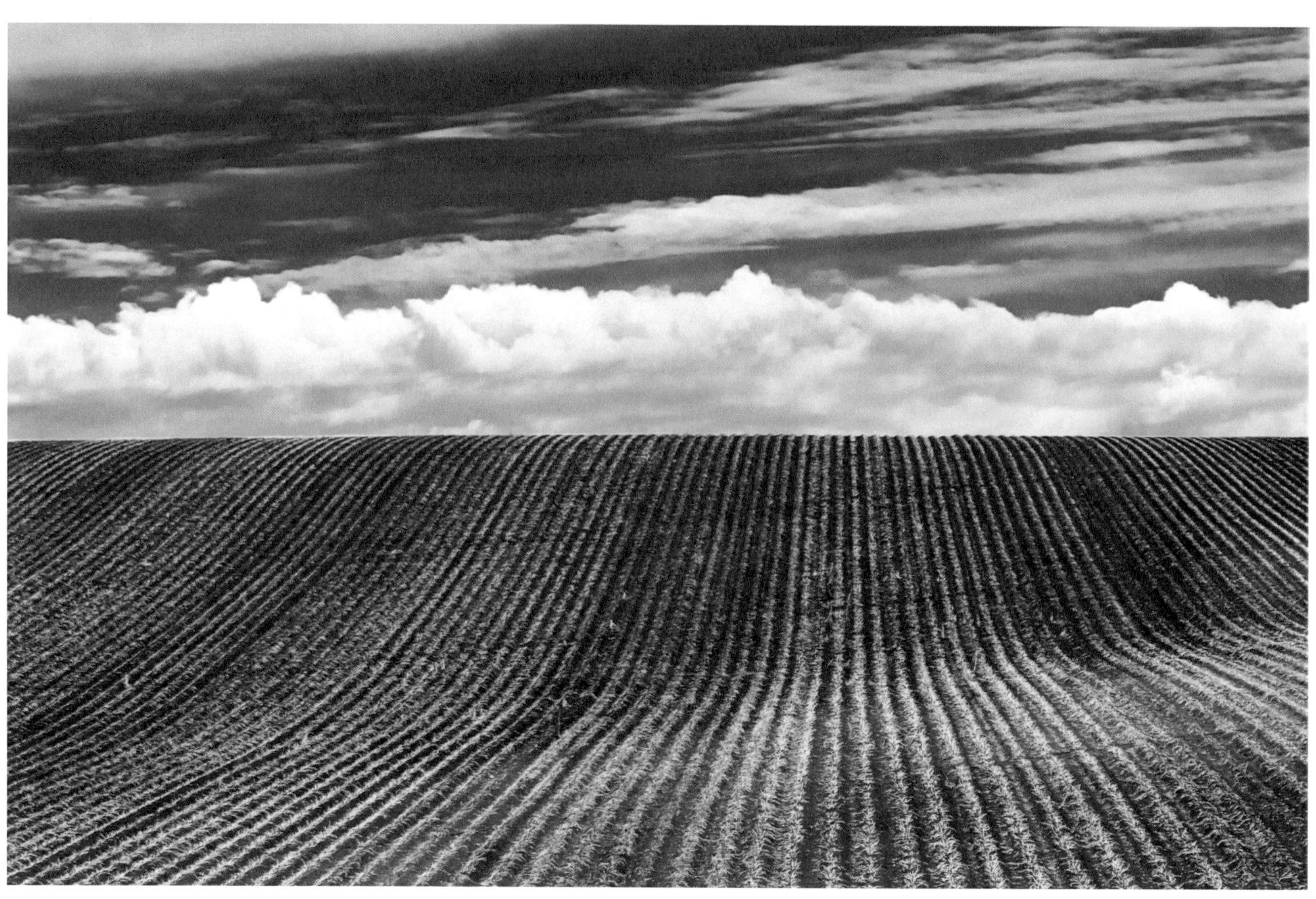

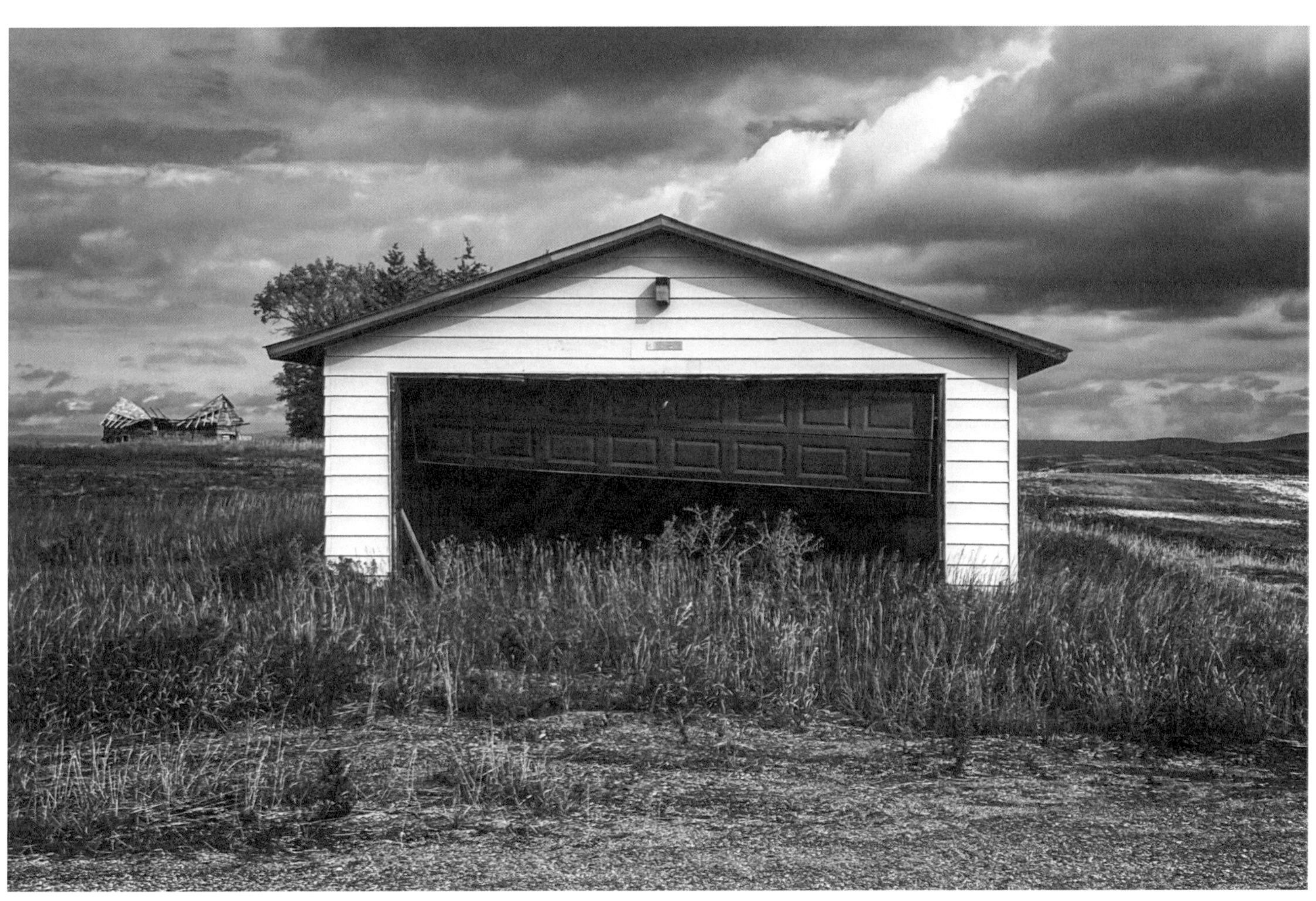

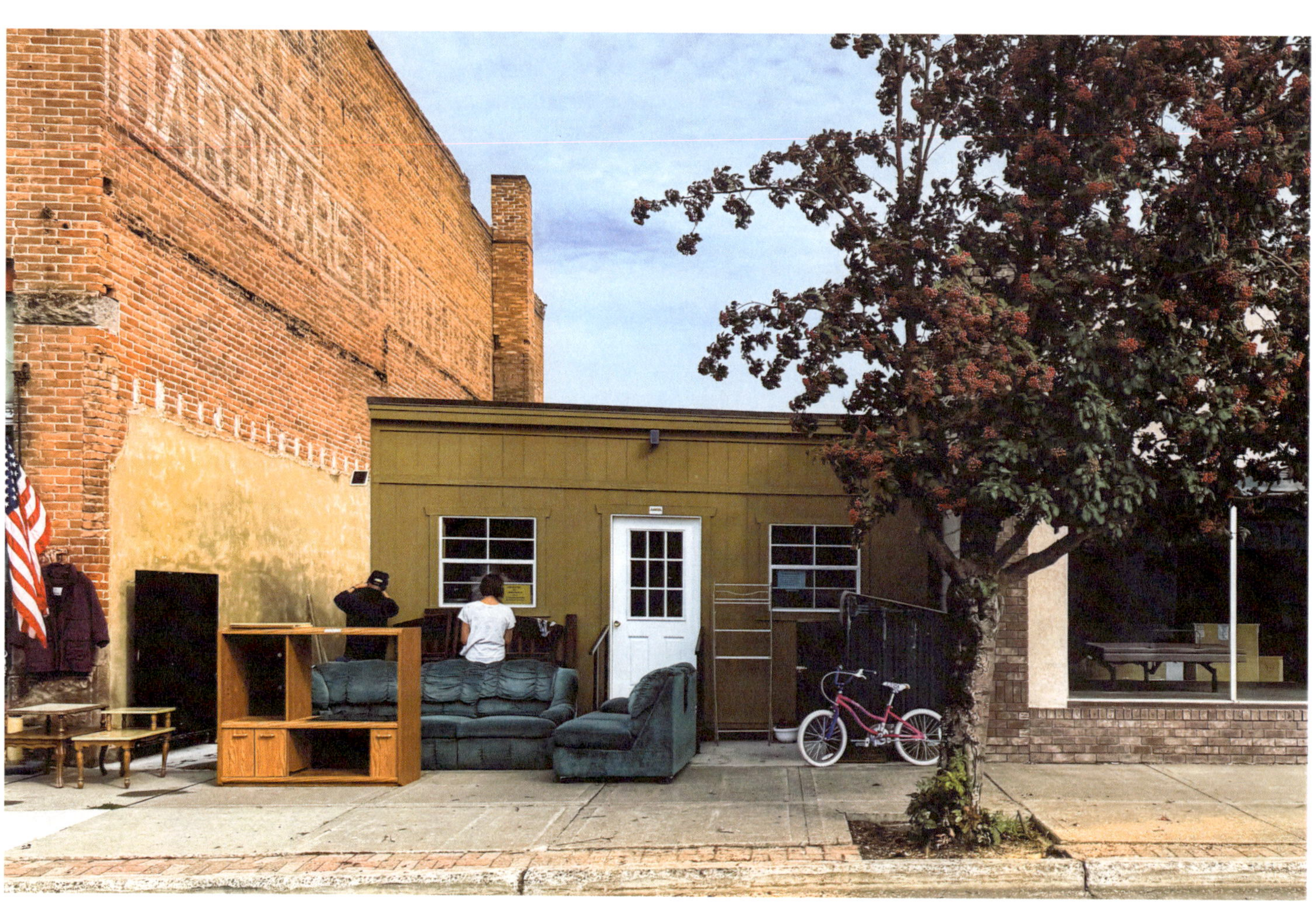

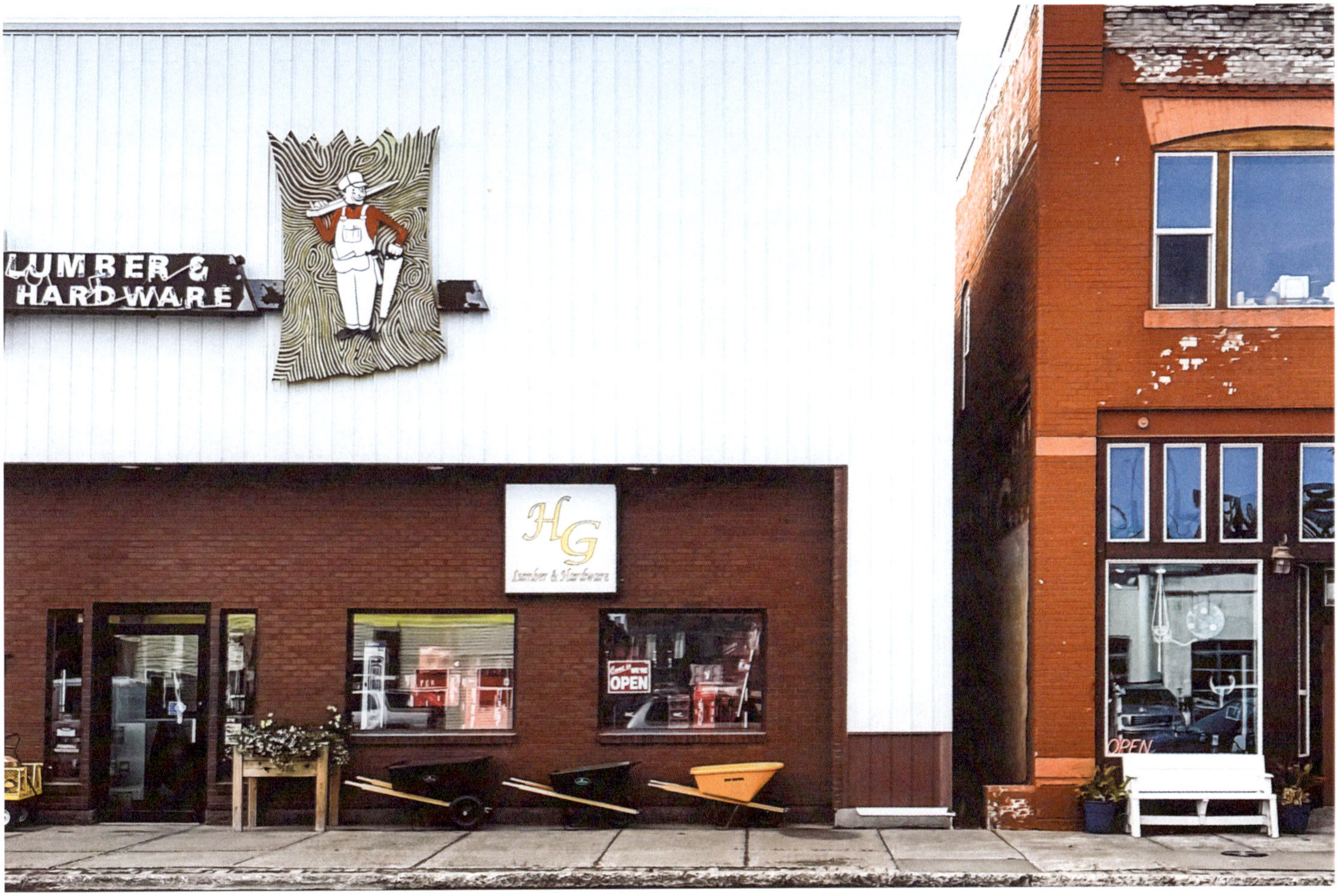

LUMBER &
HARDWARE
H
G
Lumber & Hardware
OPEN
OPEN

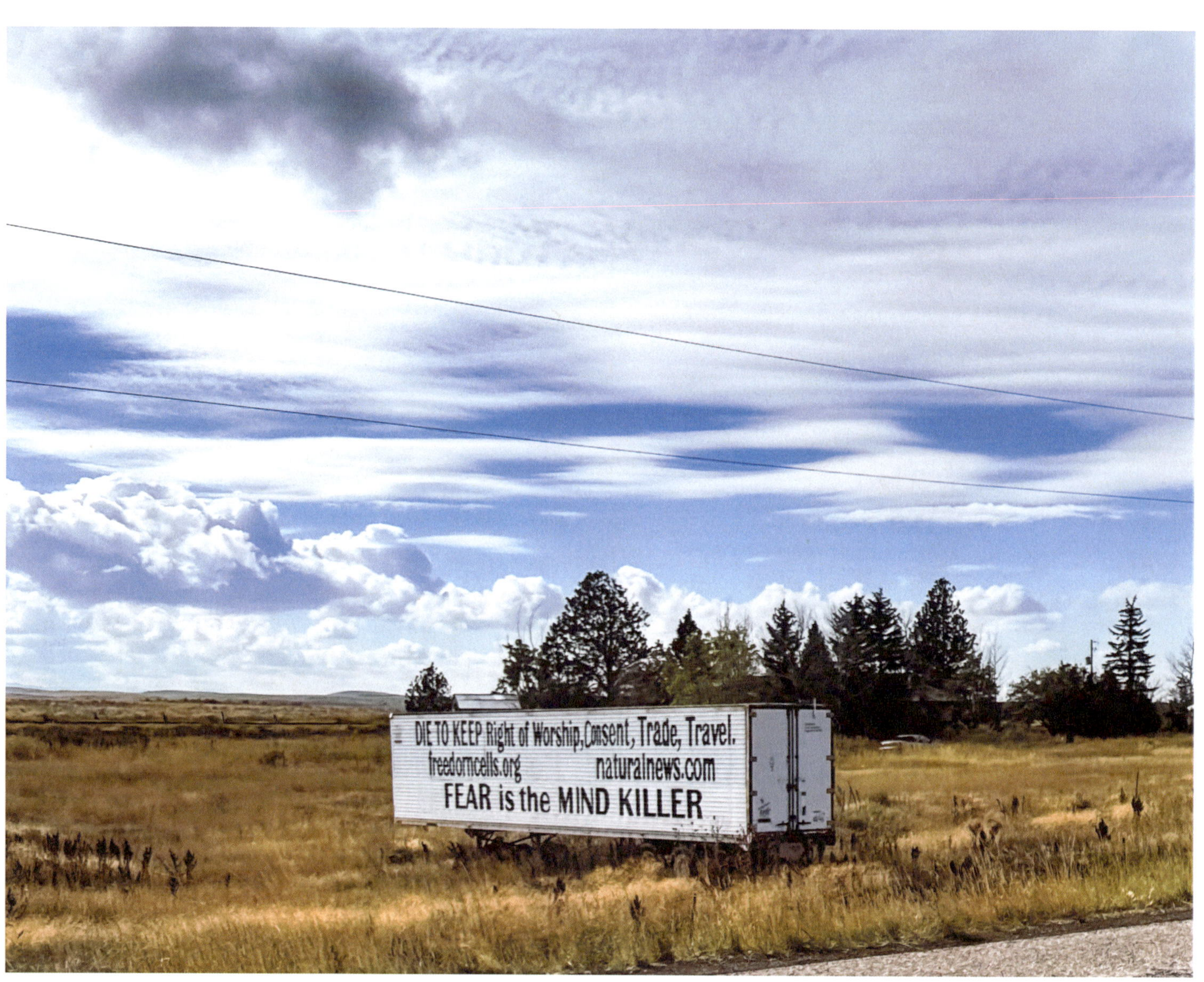

DIE TO KEEP Right of Worship,Consent, Trade, Travel.
freedomcells.org   naturalnews.com
FEAR is the MIND KILLER.

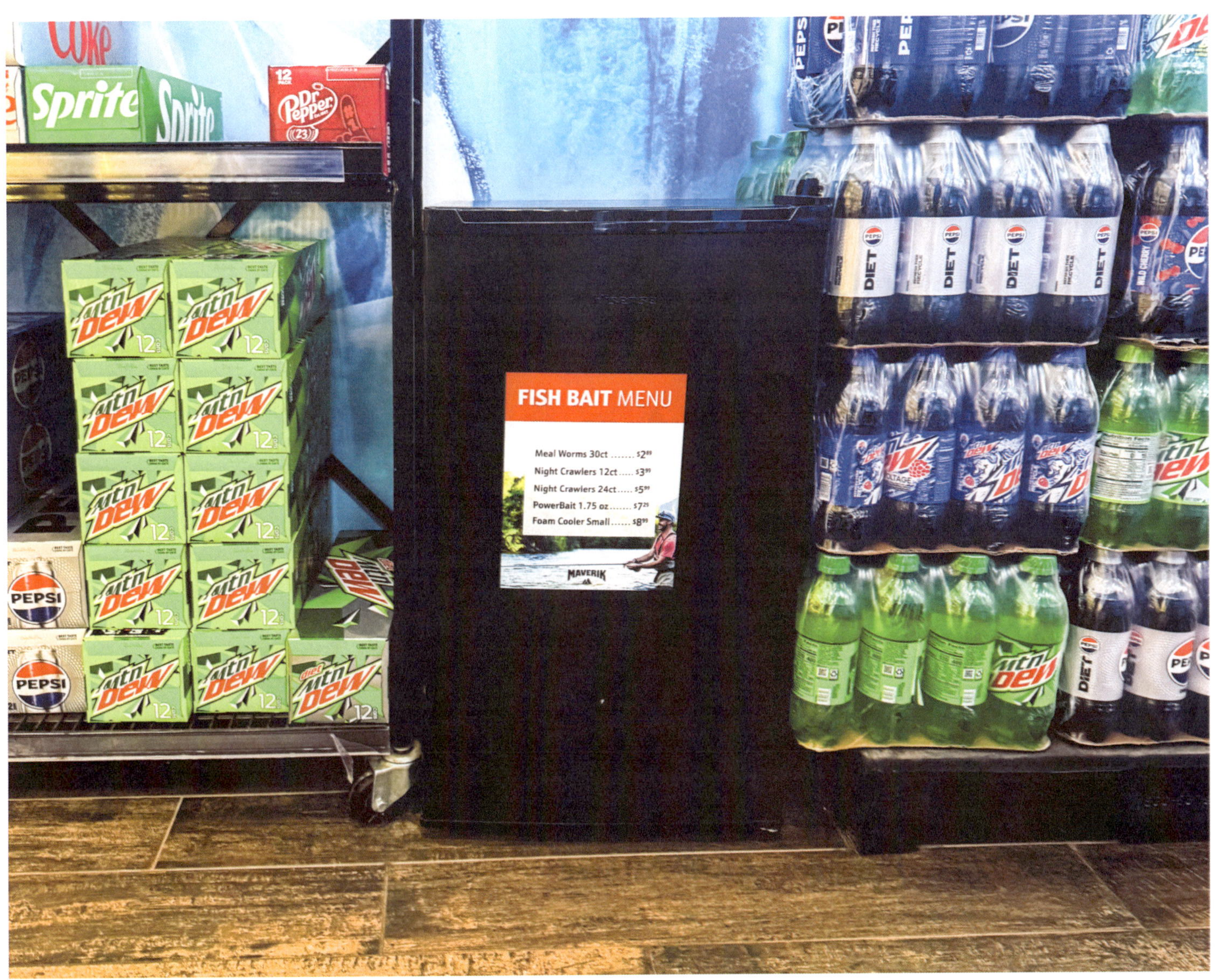
FISH BAIT MENU
Meal Worms 30ct $2.89
Night Crawlers 12ct $3.99
Night Crawlers 24ct $5.99
PowerBait 1.75 oz $7.25
Foam Cooler Small $8.99
MAVERIK

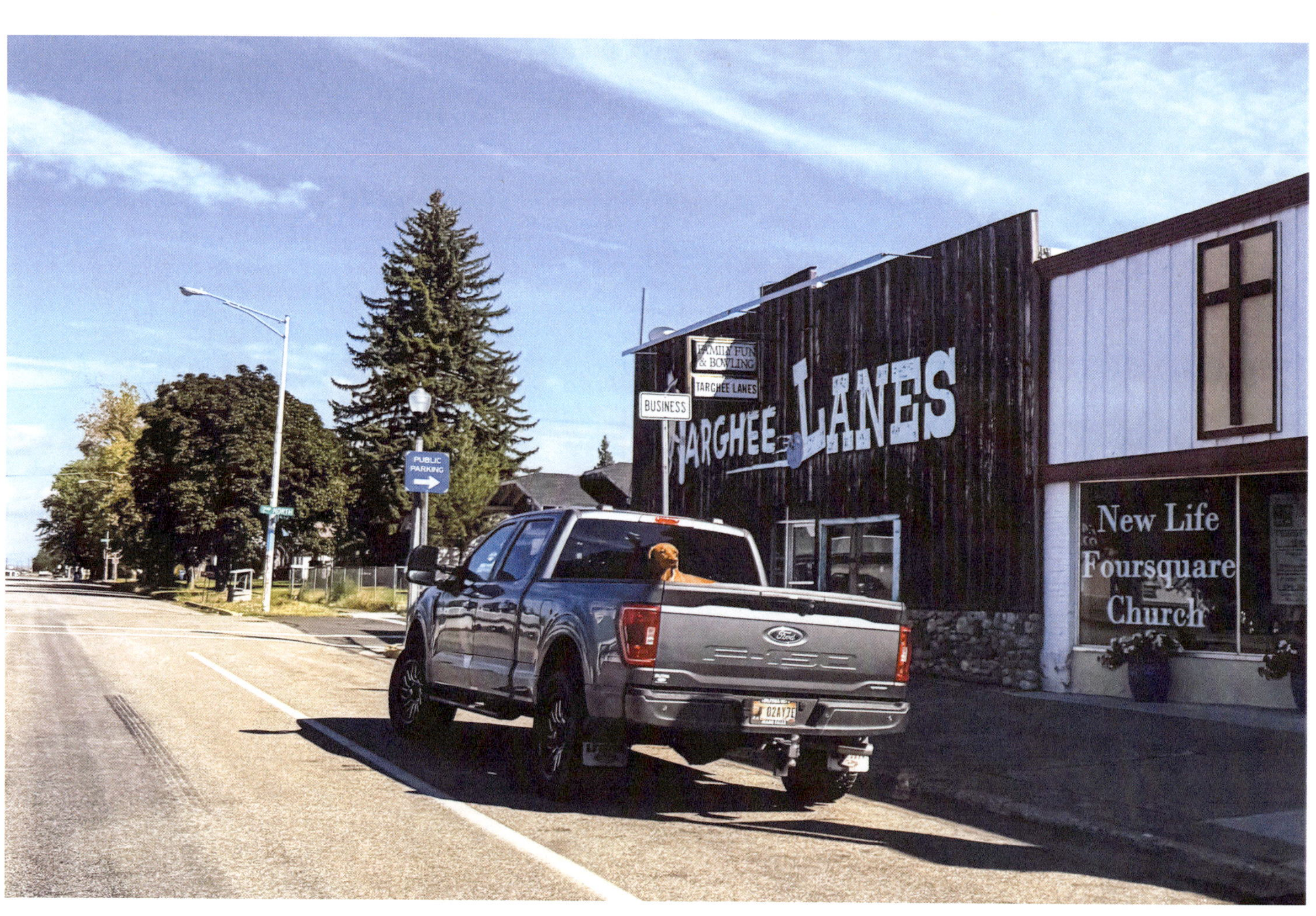
FAMILY FUN & BOWLING
TARGHEE LANES
BUSINESS
TARGHEE LANES
PUBLIC PARKING
Ford
F-150
02AY7E
New Life
Foursquare
Church

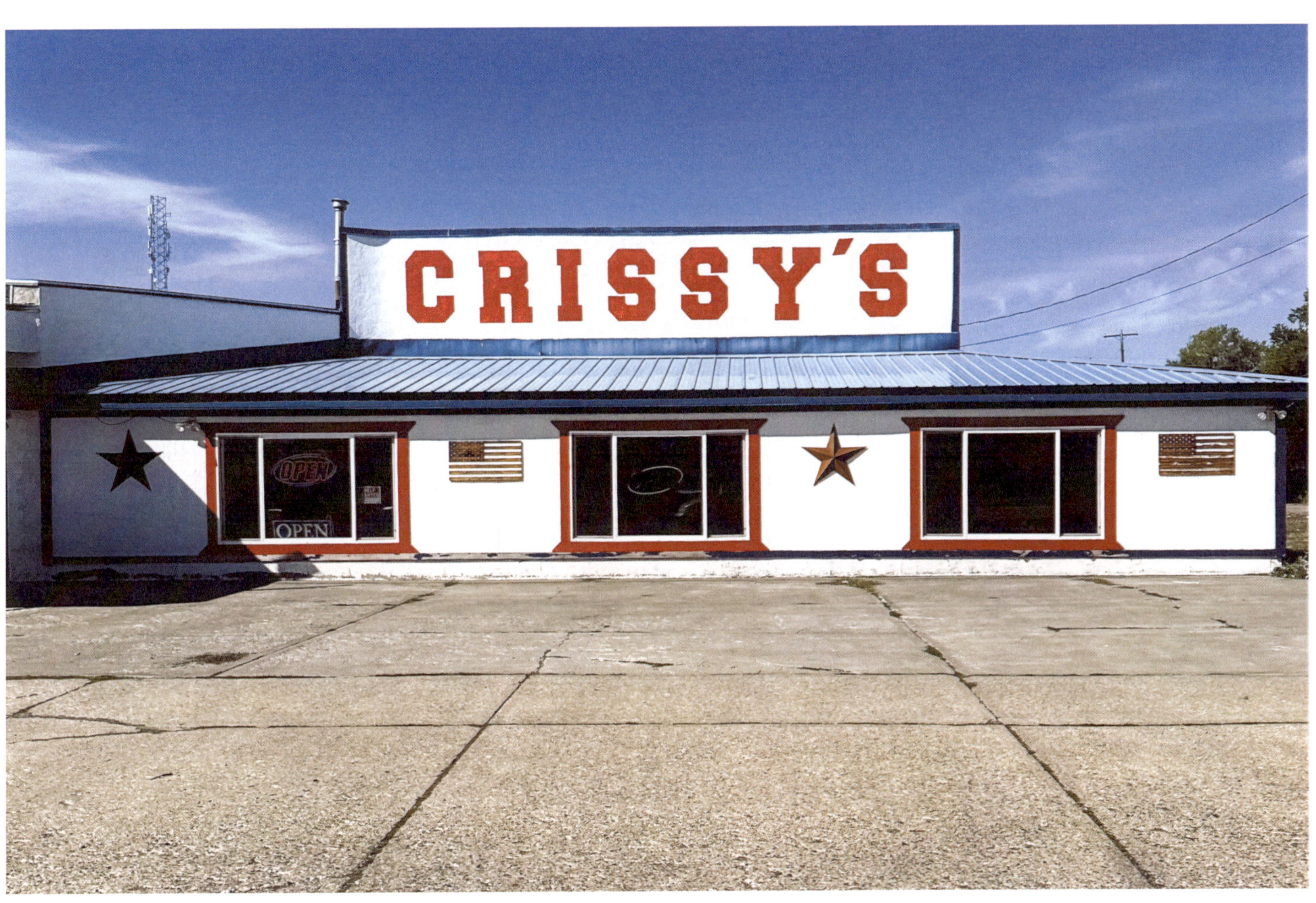

CRISSY'S
OPEN
OPEN

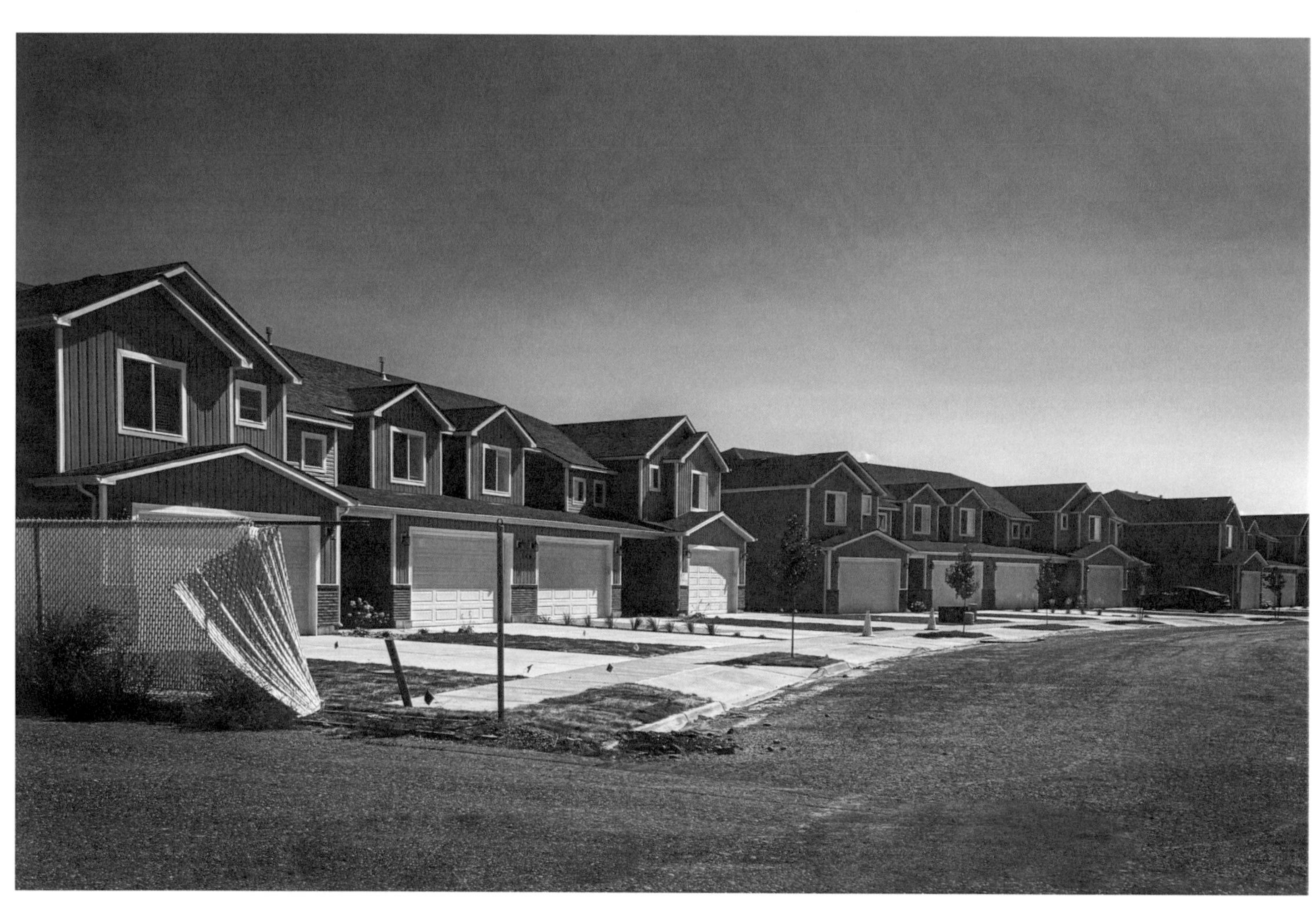

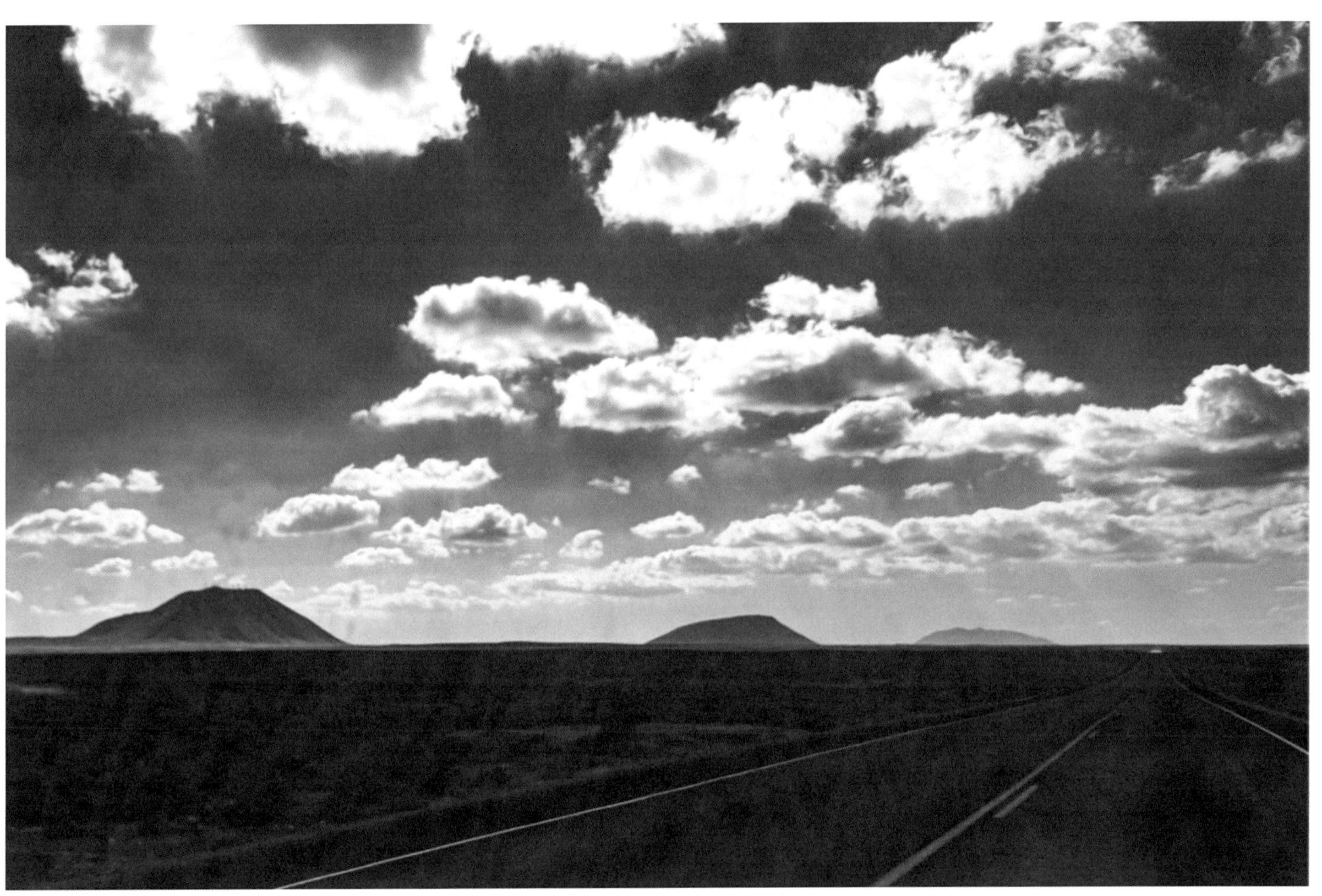

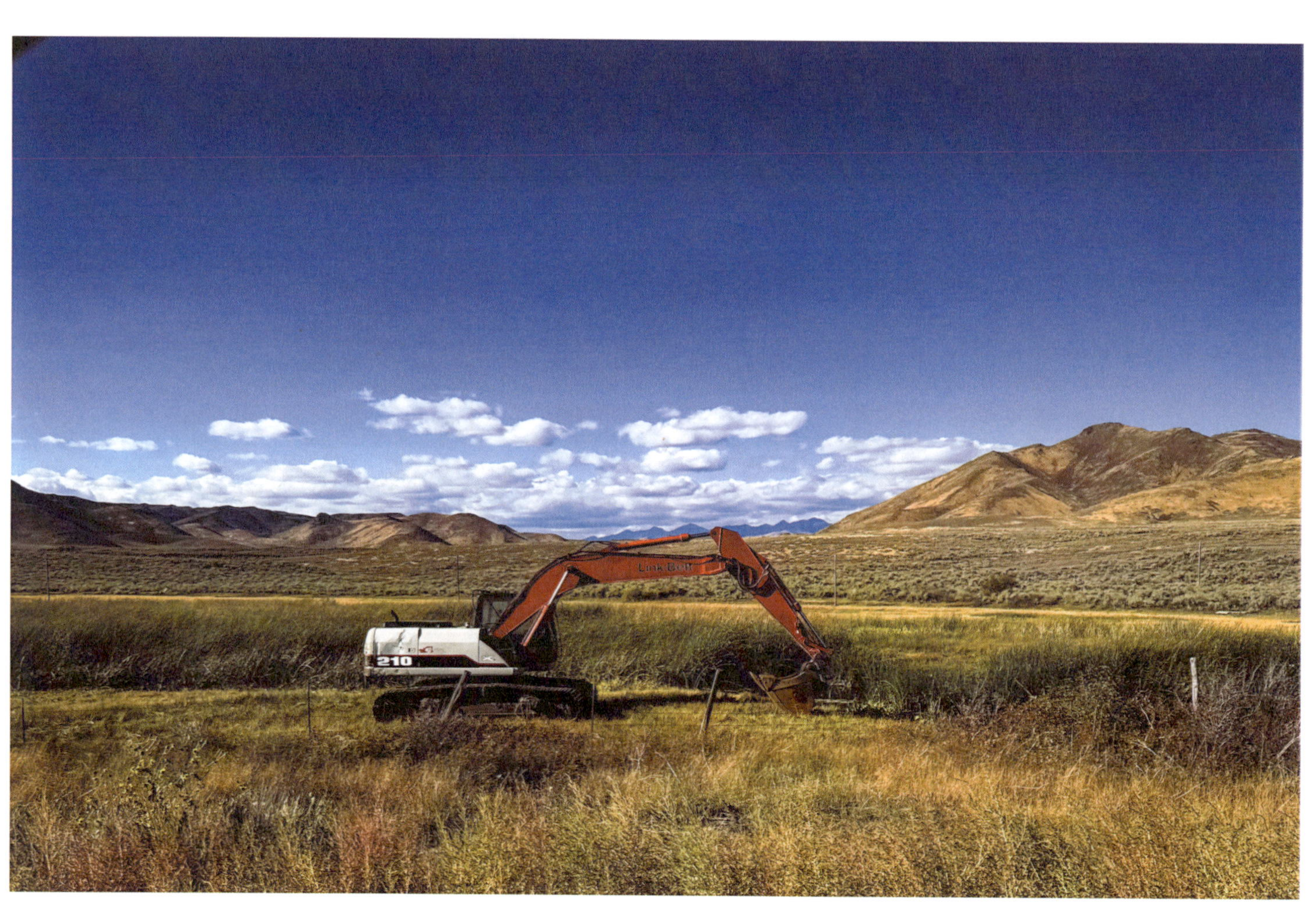
210
Link-Belt

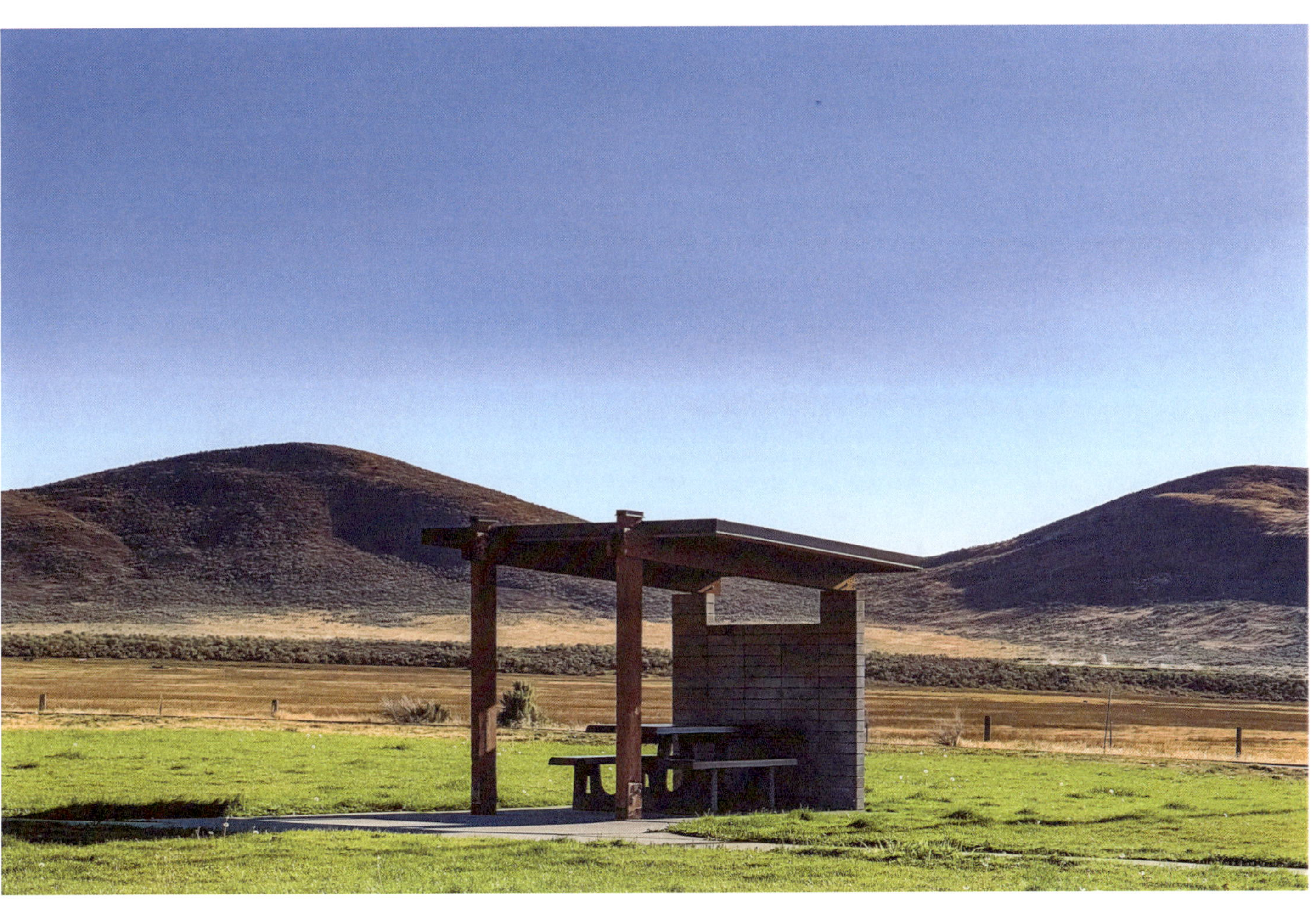

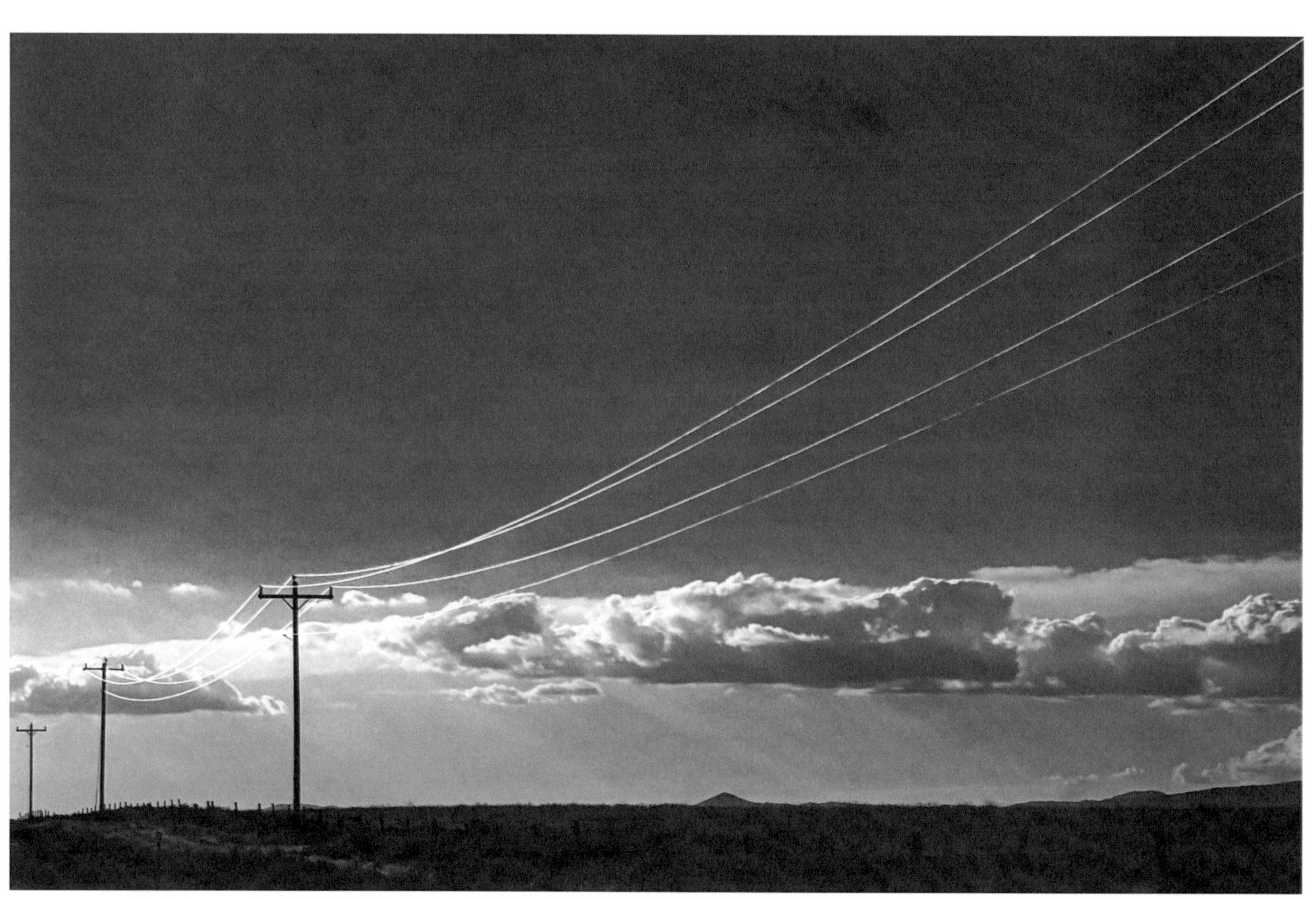

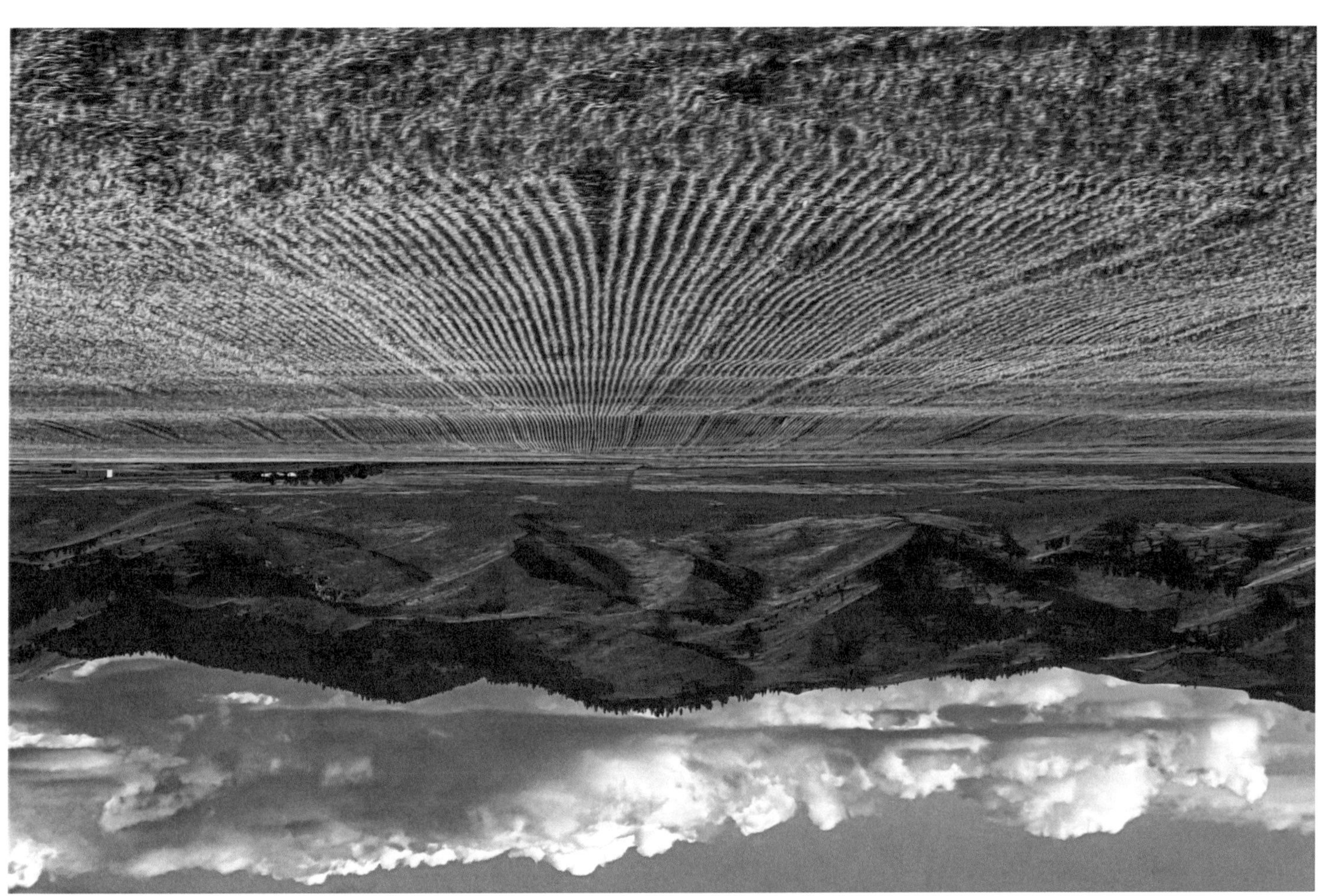

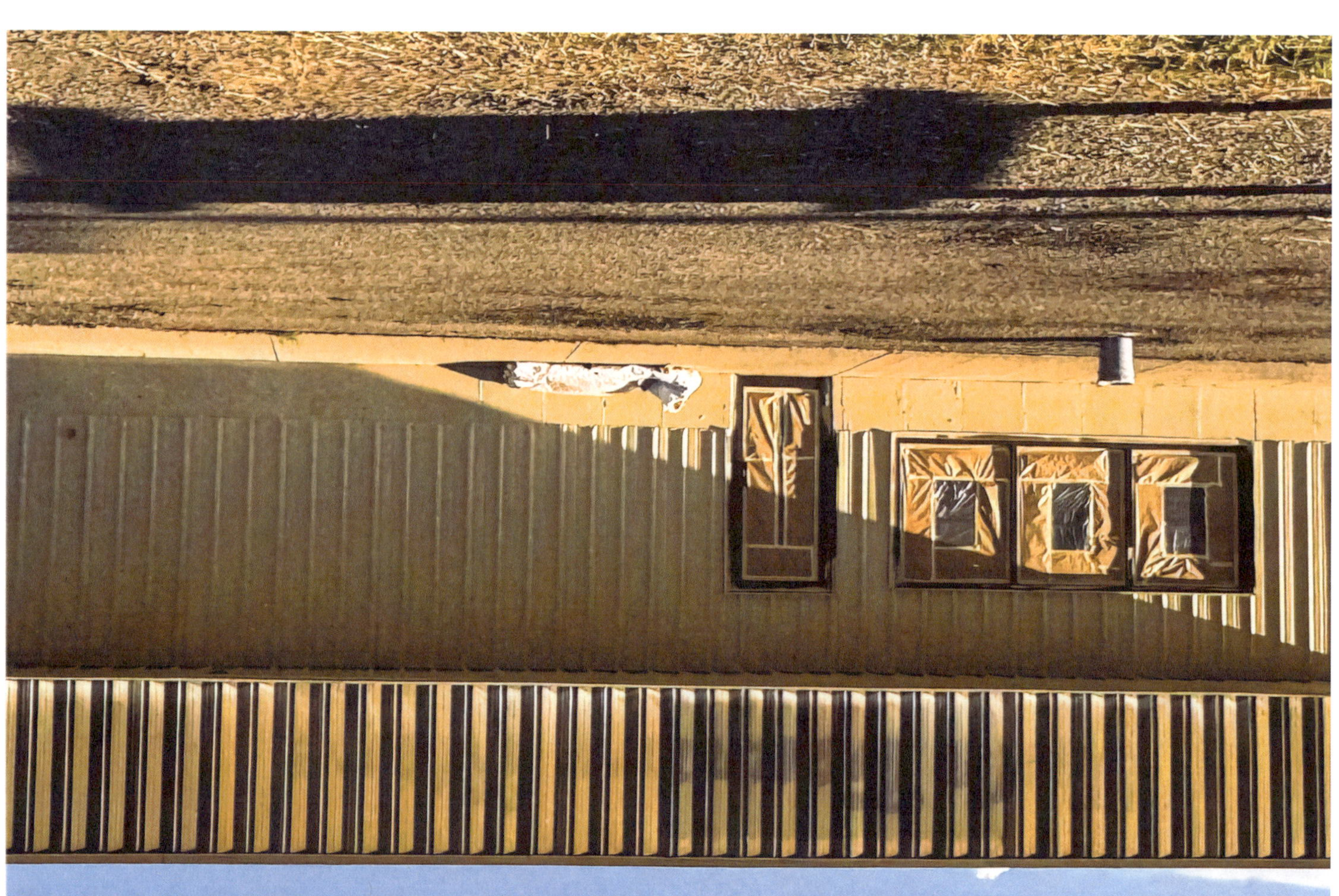

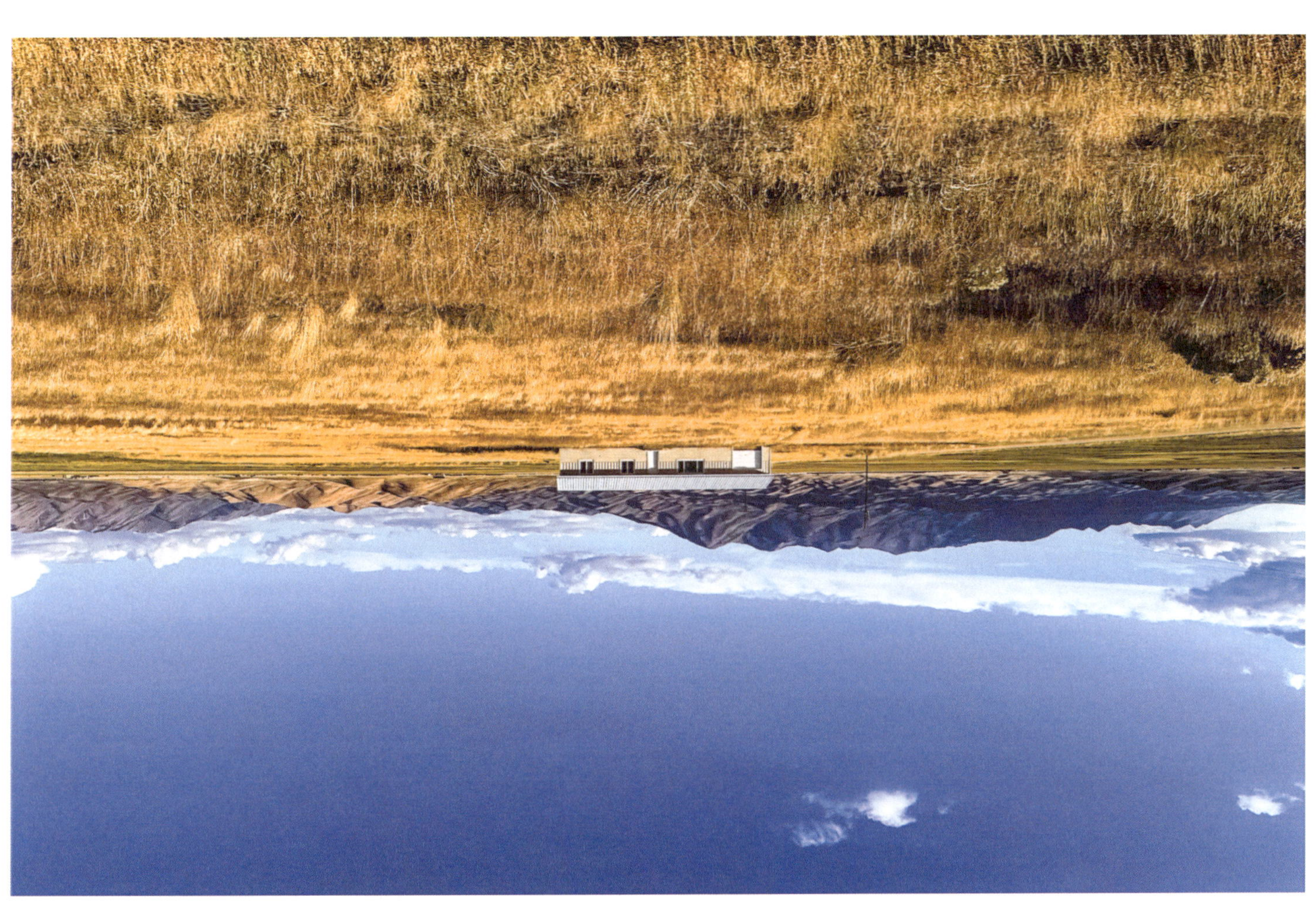

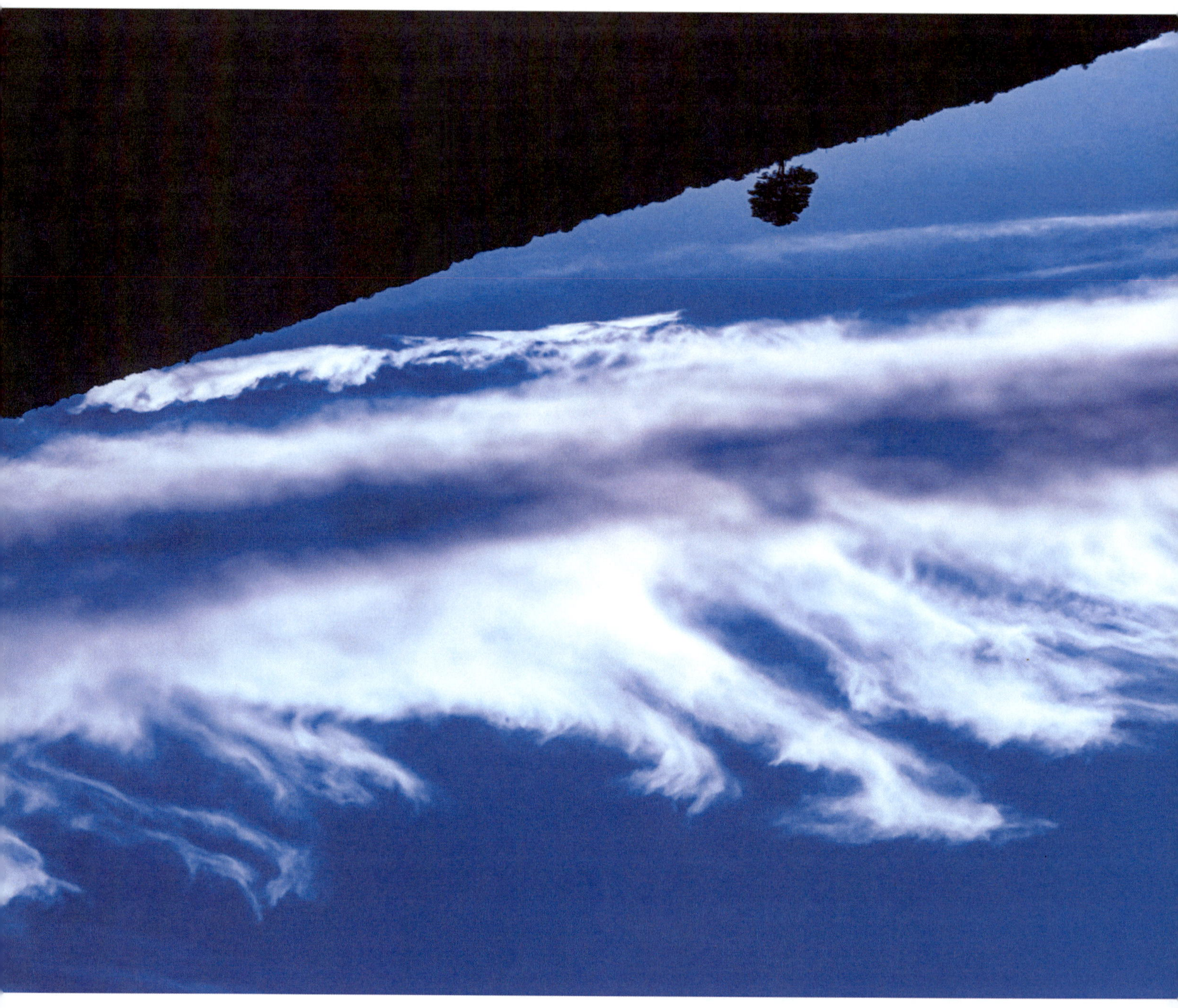